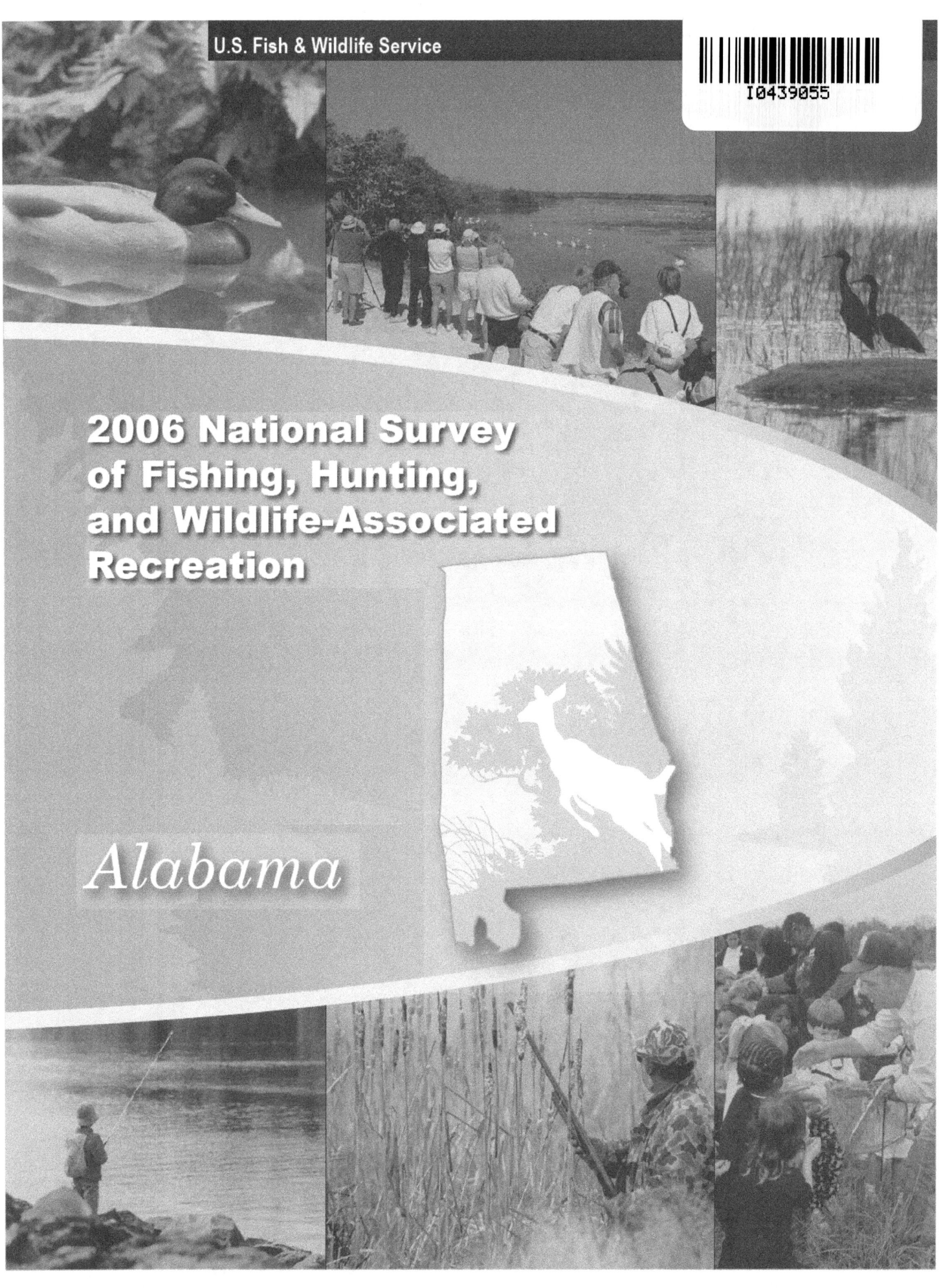

2006 National Survey of Fishing, Hunting, and Wildlife-Associated Recreation

Alabama

I0439055

FHW/06-AL
Issued November 2007

2006 National Survey of Fishing, Hunting, and Wildlife-Associated Recreation

Alabama

U.S. Department of the Interior
Dirk Kempthorne,
Secretary

U.S. Fish and Wildlife Service
H. Dale Hall,
Director

U.S. Department of Commerce
Carlos M. Gutierrez,
Secretary

Economics and Statistics Administration
Cynthia A. Glassman,
Under Secretary for Economic Affairs

U.S. CENSUS BUREAU
Charles Louis Kincannon,
Director

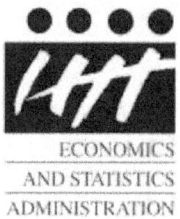

Economics and Statistics Administration

Cynthia A. Glassman,
Under Secretary for Economic Affairs

U.S. CENSUS BUREAU
Charles Louis Kincannon,
Director

U.S. Department of the Interior
Dirk Kempthorne,
Secretary

U.S. Fish and Wildlife Service
H. Dale Hall,
Director

Wildlife and Sport Fish Restoration
Rowan Gould,
Assistant Director

The U.S. Department of the Interior protects and manages the Nation's natural resources and cultural heritage; provides scientific and other information about those resources; and honors its trust responsibilities or special commitments to American Indians, Alaska Natives, and affiliated Island Communities.

The mission of the Department's U.S. Fish and Wildlife Service is working with others to conserve, protect, and enhance fish, wildlife, and their habitats for the continuing benefit of the American people. The Service is responsible for national programs of vital importance to our natural resources, including administration of the Wildlife and Sport Fish Restoration Programs. These two programs provide financial assistance to the States for projects to enhance and protect fish and wildlife resources and to assure their availability to the public for recreational purposes. Multistate grants from these programs fund the National Survey of Fishing, Hunting, and Wildlife-Associated Recreation.

Suggested Citation

U.S. Department of the Interior, Fish and Wildlife Service, and U.S. Department of Commerce, U.S. Census Bureau. 2006 National Survey of Fishing, Hunting, and Wildlife-Associated Recreation.

Contents

Highlights

Tables

Appendixes

List of Tables

Fishing and Hunting

Wildlife Watching

National Tables

Foreword

I find duck hunting with friends in a bottomland hardwood swamp or fishing with my kids on an Oregon river bolsters my spirit and reminds me why I care about conservation and our wildlife heritage.

But wildlife-associated and vital recreation—activities such as hunting, fishing, and birding—also provide significant financial support for wildlife conservation in our Nation's economy. According to information from the newest National Survey of Fishing, Hunting, and Wildlife-Associated Recreation, 87.5 million Americans spent more than $122 billion in 2006 on wildlife-related recreation. And this spending supports hundreds of thousands of jobs in industries and businesses.

The Survey is conducted every five years at the request of State fish and wildlife agencies to measure the importance of wildlife-based recreation to the American people. The 2006 Survey represents the 11th in a series that began in 1955. Developed in collaboration with the States, the Association of Fish and Wildlife Agencies, and national conservation organizations, the Survey has become one of the most important sources of information on fish and wildlife-related recreation in the United States.

In the 75-year history of the Sport Fish and Wildlife Restoration Programs, excise taxes on firearms, ammunition, archery, and angling equipment have generated a cumulative total of more than $10 billion for wildlife conservation efforts by State and Territorial wildlife agencies for fish and wildlife management.

My thanks go to the men and women who took time to participate in the survey, as well as to the State fish and wildlife agencies for their financial support through the Multistate State Conservation Grant Programs. Without that support, the 2006 Survey would never have been possible.

I am comforted to know that my children and all Americans will have the opportunity to appreciate our Nation's rich wildlife tradition. Along with a record number of Americans, we continue to enjoy wildlife. We are laying the foundation for conservation's future.

H. Dale Hall

H. Dale Hall
Director, U.S. Fish and Wildlife Service

Survey Background and Method

The National Survey of Fishing, Hunting, and Wildlife-Associated Recreation (Survey) has been conducted since 1955 and is one of the oldest and most comprehensive continuing recreation surveys. The Survey collects information on the number of anglers, hunters, and wildlife watchers; how often they participate; and how much they spend on their activities in the United States.

Preparations for the 2006 Survey began in 2004 when the Association of Fish and Wildlife Agencies (AFWA) recommended that the Fish and Wildlife Service conduct the 11th Survey of wildlife-related recreation. Funding came from the Multistate Conservation Grant Programs, authorized by Sport Fish and Wildlife Restoration Acts, as amended.

We consulted with State and Federal agencies and nongovernmental organizations such as the Wildlife Management Institute and American Sportfishing Association to determine survey content. Other sportspersons' organizations and conservation groups, industry representatives, and researchers also provided valuable advice.

Four regional technical committees were set up under the auspices of the AFWA to ensure that State fish and wildlife agencies had an opportunity to participate in all phases of survey planning and design. The committees were made up of agency representatives.

Data collection for the Survey was carried out by the U.S. Census Bureau in two phases. The first phase was the screen which began in April 2006. During this phase the Census Bureau interviewed a sample of 85,000 households nationwide to determine who in the household had fished, hunted, or wildlife watched in 2005, and who had engaged or planned to engage in those activities in 2006. In most cases, one adult household member provided information for all members. The screen primarily covered 2005 activities while the next, more in-depth phase covered 2006 activities. For more information on 2005 data, refer to Appendix B.

The second phase of data collection consisted of three detailed interview waves. The first began in April 2006 concurrent with the screen, the second in September 2006, and the last in January 2007. Interviews were conducted with samples of likely anglers, hunters, and wildlife watchers who were identified in the initial screening phase. Interviews were conducted primarily by phone, with in-person interviews for respondents who could not be reached by phone. Respondents in the second survey phase were limited to those who were at least 16 years old. Each respondent provided information pertaining only to his or her activities and expenditures. Sample sizes were designed to provide statistically reliable results at the state level. Information on sampling procedures, sample sizes, and response rates is found in Appendix D.

Comparability With Previous Surveys

The 2006 Survey questions and methodology were similar to those used in the 2001, 1996, and 1991 Surveys. Therefore, the estimates are comparable.

The methodology of these Surveys did differ importantly from the 1985 and 1980 Surveys, so these estimates are not directly comparable to those of earlier surveys. Changes in methodology included reducing the recall period over which respondents had to report their activities and expenditures. Previous Surveys used a 12-month recall period, which resulted in greater reporting bias. Research found that the amount of activity and expenditures reported in 12-month recall surveys was overestimated in comparison with that reported using shorter recall periods.

Highlights

Introduction

The National Survey of Fishing, Hunting, and Wildlife-Associated Recreation reports results from interviews with U.S. residents about their fishing, hunting, and wildlife watching. This report focuses on 2006 participation and expenditures of persons 16 years of age and older.

The Survey is a snapshot of one year. The information it collected tells us how many people participated and how much they spent on their activities in the State in 2006. It does not tell us how many anglers, hunters, and wildlife watchers there were because many do not participate every year. For example, based on information collected by the Survey's household screen and detailed phase, we can estimate that about 33 percent more anglers and hunters participated nationally in at least 1 of the 4 years prior to the survey year 2006.

In addition to 2006 estimates, we also provide trend information in the Highlights section and Appendix C of the report. The 2006 numbers reported can be compared with those in the 1991, 1996, and 2001 Survey reports because they used similar methodologies. The 2006 estimates should not be directly compared with results from Surveys conducted earlier than 1991 because of changes in methodology to improve accuracy.

The report also provides information on participation in wildlife recreation in 2005, particularly of persons 6 to 15 years of age. The 2005 information is provided in Appendix B. Information about the Survey's scope and coverage is in Appendix D. The remainder of this section defines important terms used in the Survey.

This report does not provide information about the State's wildlife resources. That, and additional information on wildlife-related recreation, may be obtained from State fish and wildlife agencies. The Association of Fish and Wildlife Agencies can provide the addresses and telephone numbers of those agencies. The Association's Web site is <www.fishwildlife.org>.

Wildlife-Associated Recreation

Wildlife-associated recreation is fishing, hunting, and wildlife-watching activities. These categories are not mutually exclusive because many individuals participated in more than one activity. Wildlife-associated recreation is reported in two major categories: (1) fishing and hunting and (2) wildlife watching, which includes observing, photographing, and feeding fish or wildlife.

Fishing and Hunting

This Survey reports information about residents of the United States who fished or hunted in 2006, regardless of whether they were licensed. The fishing and hunting sections report information for three groups: (1) sportspersons, (2) anglers, and (3) hunters.

Sportspersons

Sportspersons are those who fished or hunted. Individuals who fished or hunted commercially in 2006 are reported as sportspersons only if they also fished or hunted for recreation. The sportspersons group is composed of three subgroups, as shown in the diagram on this page: (1) those that fished and hunted, (2) those that only fished, and (3) those that only hunted.

The total number of sportspersons is equal to the sum of people who only fished, only hunted, and both hunted and fished. It is not the sum of all anglers and all hunters because those people who both fished and hunted are included in both the angler and hunter population and would be incorrectly counted twice.

Sportspersons

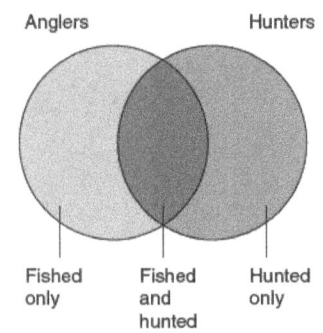

Anglers   Hunters

Fished only   Fished and hunted   Hunted only

Anglers

Anglers are sportspersons who only fished plus those who fished and hunted. Anglers include not only licensed hook and line anglers, but also those who have no license and those who use special methods such as fishing with spears.

Three types of fishing are reported: (1) freshwater, excluding the Great Lakes, (2) Great Lakes, and (3) saltwater. Since many anglers participated in more than one type of fishing, the total number of anglers is less than the sum of the three types of fishing.

Hunters

Hunters are sportspersons who only hunted plus those who hunted and fished. Hunters include not only licensed hunters using rifles and shotguns but also those who had no license and those who hunted with a bow and arrow, primitive firearm, or pistol or handgun.

Four types of hunting are reported: (1) big game, (2) small game, (3) migratory bird, and (4) other animals. Since many hunters participated in more than one type of hunting, the sum of hunters for big game, small game, migratory bird, and other animals exceeds the total number of hunters.

Wildlife Watchers

Since 1980, the National Survey has included information on wildlife-watching activities in addition to fishing and hunting. The 1991, 1996, 2001, and 2006 Surveys, unlike the 1980 and 1985 Surveys, collected data only for activities where the *primary* purpose was wildlife watching. The 1980 and 1985 Surveys included estimates of unplanned wildlife watching around the home and while on trips taken for another purpose.

The 2006 Survey uses a strict definition of wildlife watching. Participants must either take a "special interest" in wildlife around their homes or take a trip for the "primary purpose" of wildlife watching. Secondary wildlife watching, such as incidentally observing wildlife while pleasure driving, is not included.

Two types of wildlife watching are reported: (1) away-from-home (formerly nonresidential) activities and (2) around-the-home (formerly residential) activities. Because some people participated in more than one type of wildlife watching, the sum of participants in each type will be greater than the total number of wildlife watchers. The two types of wildlife-watching activity are explained next.

Away-From-Home Wildlife Watching

This group includes persons who took trips or outings of at least 1 mile from home for the primary purpose of observing, feeding, or photographing fish and wildlife. Trips to fish, hunt, or scout and trips to zoos, circuses, aquariums, and museums are not considered wildlife-watching activities.

Around-the-Home Wildlife Watching

This group includes those who participated within 1 mile of home and involves one or more of the following: (1) closely observing or trying to identify birds or other wildlife; (2) photographing wildlife; (3) feeding birds or other wildlife; (4) maintaining natural areas of at least 1/4 acre where benefit to wildlife is the primary concern; (5) maintaining plantings (shrubs, agricultural crops, etc.) where benefit to wildlife is the primary concern; or (6) visiting public parks within 1 mile of home for the primary purpose of observing, feeding, or photographing wildlife.

2006 Alabama Summary

Activities in Alabama by Residents and Nonresidents

Fishing

Anglers	**806,000**
Days of fishing	13,708,000
Average days per angler	17
Total expenditures	$699,532,000
Trip-related	$417,279,000
Equipment and other	$282,253,000
Average per angler	$864
Average trip expenditure per day	$30

Hunting

Hunters	**391,000**
Days of hunting	8,649,000
Average days per hunter	22
Total expenditures	$678,024,000
Trip-related	$239,398,000
Equipment and other	$438,626,000
Average per hunter	$1,724
Average trip expenditure per day	$28

Wildlife Watching

Total wildlife-watching participants	**1,161,000**
Away-from-home participants	471,000
Around-the-home participants	989,000
Days of participation away from home	4,023,000
Average days of participation away from home	9
Total expenditures	$450,004,000
Trip-related	$151,665,000
Equipment and other	$298,339,000
Average per participant	$377
Average trip expenditure per day	$38

Activities in Alabama by Nonresidents

Fishing

Anglers	**206,000**
Days of fishing	1,022,000
Average days per angler	5
Total expenditures	$129,540,000
Trip-related	$123,311,000
Equipment and other	$6,229,000
Average per angler	$628
Average trip expenditure per day	$121

Hunting

Hunters	**81,000**
Days of hunting	1,039,000
Average days per hunter	13
Total expenditures	$163,638,000
Trip-related	$88,144,000
Equipment and other	$75,494,000
Average per hunter	$2,019
Average trip expenditure per day	$85

Wildlife Watching

Total wildlife-watching participants	**156,000**
Away-from-home participants	156,000
Around-the-home participants	(X)
Days of participation away from home	659,000
Average days of participation away from home	4
Total expenditures	$64,908,000
Trip-related	$58,245,000
Equipment and other	$6,663,000
Average per participant	$374
Average trip expenditure per day	$88

(X) Not applicable.

Activities in Alabama by Residents

Fishing

Anglers	**600,000**
Days of fishing	12,686,000
Average days per angler	21
Total expenditures	$569,992,000
Trip-related	$293,968,000
Equipment and other	$276,024,000
Average per angler	$950
Average trip expenditure per day	$23

Hunting

Hunters	**310,000**
Days of hunting	7,609,000
Average days per hunter	25
Total expenditures	$514,386,000
Trip-related	$151,254,000
Equipment and other	$363,132,000
Average per hunter	$1,660
Average trip expenditure per day	$20

Wildlife Watching

Total wildlife-watching participants	**1,005,000**
Away-from-home participants	315,000
Around-the-home participants	989,000
Days of participation away from home	3,365,000
Average days of participation away from home	11
Total expenditures	$385,096,000
Trip-related	$93,420,000
Equipment and other	$291,676,000
Average per participant	$383
Average trip expenditure per day	$28

Activities by Alabama Residents Both Inside and Outside Alabama

Fishing

Anglers	**628,000**
Days of fishing	13,164,000
Average days per angler	21
Total expenditures	$791,187,000
Trip-related	$360,565,000
Equipment and other	$430,622,000
Average per angler	$1,260
Average trip expenditure per day	$27

Hunting

Hunters	**312,000**
Days of hunting	8,032,000
Average days per hunter	26
Total expenditures	$596,485,000
Trip-related	$214,012,000
Equipment and other	$382,473,000
Average per hunter	$1,912
Average trip expenditure per day	$27

Wildlife Watching

Total wildlife-watching participants	**1,006,000**
Away-from-home participants	348,000
Around-the-home participants	989,000
Days of participation away from home	7,488,000
Average days of participation away from home	22
Total expenditures	$493,849,000
Trip-related	$198,132,000
Equipment and other	$295,717,000
Average per participant	$491
Average trip expenditure per day	$26

Wildlife-Associated Recreation

Participation in Alabama

The 2006 Survey found that 1.7 million Alabama residents and nonresidents 16 years old and older fished, hunted, or wildlife watched in Alabama. Of the total number of participants, 806 thousand fished, 391 thousand hunted, and 1.2 million participated in wildlife-watching activities, which includes observing, feeding, and photographing wildlife. The sum of anglers, hunters, and wildlife watchers exceeds the total number of participants in wildlife-related recreation because many individuals engaged in more than one wildlife-related activity.

Participation by 6-to-15-Year-Old Alabama Residents

The focus of the National Survey is on the activity of participants 16 years old and older. However, the activity of 6- to 15-year-olds can be calculated using the screening data covering the year 2005. It is assumed for estimation purposes that the relative activity levels of 6-to-15-year-old participants and participants 16 years old and older remained the same in 2005 and 2006. Based on this assumption, in addition to the 628,000 resident anglers 16 years old and older in Alabama, there were 155,000 resident anglers 6 to 15 years old. Also, there were 312,000 Alabamians 16 years old and older and 66,000 Alabamians 6 to 15 years old who hunted. Finally, there were 1.0 million Alabamians 16 years old and older and 162,000 Alabamians 6 to 15 years old who wildlife watched. Further information on 6- to 15-year-olds is provided in Appendix B.

Expenditures in Alabama

In 2006, state residents and nonresidents spent $2.2 billion on wildlife recreation in Alabama. Of that total, trip-related expenditures were $808 million and equipment purchases totaled $1.1 billion. The remaining $231 million was spent on licenses, contributions, land ownership and leasing, and other items.

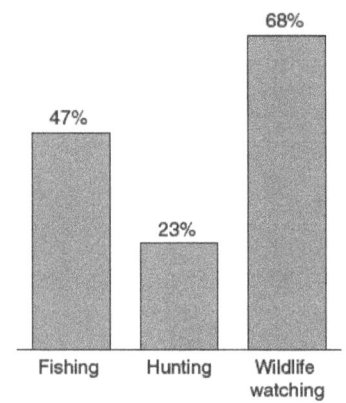

Percent of Total Participants by Activity
(Total: 1.7 million participants)

- Fishing — 47%
- Hunting — 23%
- Wildlife watching — 68%

Participants in Wildlife-Associated Recreation in Alabama: 2006
(U.S. residents 16 years old and older)

Total	1.7 million
Sportspersons	
Total	962 thousand
Anglers	806 thousand
Hunters	391 thousand
Wildlife Watchers	
Total	1.2 million
Away from home.........................	471 thousand
Around the home.........................	989 thousand

Note: Detail does not add to total because of multiple responses.

Source: Tables 3, 24, and 39.

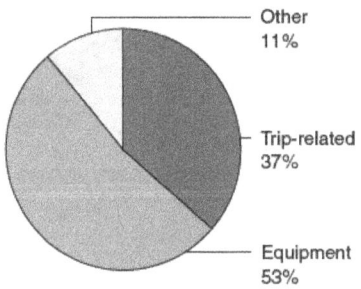

Wildlife-Associated Recreation Expenditures in Alabama
(Total: $2.2 billion)

- Other 11%
- Trip-related 37%
- Equipment 53%

Sportspersons

In 2006, 962 thousand state resident and nonresident sportspersons 16 years old and older fished or hunted in Alabama. This group comprised 806 thousand anglers (84 percent of all sportspersons) and 391 thousand hunters (41 percent of all sportspersons). Among the 962 thousand sportspersons who fished or hunted in the state, 571 thousand (59 percent) fished but did not hunt in Alabama. Another 156 thousand (16 percent) hunted but did not fish there. The remaining 235 thousand (24 percent) fished and hunted in Alabama in 2006.

Sportspersons' Participation in Alabama
(State residents and nonresidents 16 years old and older)

Sportspersons (fished or hunted)	**962 thousand**
Anglers	**806 thousand**
Fished only	571 thousand
Fished and hunted	235 thousand
Hunters.	**391 thousand**
Hunted only.	156 thousand
Hunted and fished	235 thousand

Note: Detail does not add to total because of multiple responses.

Source: Table 1.

Anglers

Participants and Days of Fishing

In 2006, 806 thousand state residents and nonresidents 16 years old and older fished in Alabama. Of this total, 600 thousand anglers (74 percent) were state residents and 206 thousand anglers (26 percent) were nonresidents. Anglers fished a total of 13.7 million days in Alabama—an average of 17 days per angler. State residents fished 12.7 million days—93 percent of all fishing days in Alabama. Nonresidents fished 1 million days in Alabama—7 percent of all fishing days in the state.

A large majority of Alabama residents who fished anywhere in the United States did so in their resident state. There were 628 thousand Alabama residents 16 years old and older who fished in the United States in 2006 for a total of 13.2 million days. An estimated 96 percent of all Alabama residents who fished did so in their home state. Of all fishing days by Alabama residents, 96 percent or 12.7 million were in their home state.

Some state residents fished in states other than Alabama. In 2006, 107 thousand Alabama residents fished in other states—17 percent of all residents fishing in any state. They fished 600 thousand days as nonresidents, representing 5 percent of all days fished by Alabama residents. For further details about fishing in Alabama, see Table 3.

Anglers in Alabama
(State residents and nonresidents 16 years old and older)

Anglers	**806 thousand**
Resident	600 thousand
Nonresident	206 thousand
Days of fishing	**13.7 million**
Resident	12.7 million
Nonresident	1.0 million

Source: Table 3.

In State/Out of State
(State residents 16 years old and older)

Alabama anglers	**628 thousand**
In Alabama	600 thousand
In other states	107 thousand
Days of fishing	**13.2 million**
In Alabama	12.7 million
In other states	600 thousand

Note: Detail does not add to total because of multiple responses.

Source: Table 3.

Fishing Expenditures in Alabama

All fishing-related expenditures in Alabama totaled $700 million in 2006. Trip-related expenditures, including food and lodging, transportation, and other expenses totaled $417 million—60 percent of all fishing expenditures. Expenditures for food and lodging were $126 million and transportation expenditures were $101 million. Other trip expenses, such as equipment rental, bait, and cooking fuel, totaled $190 million. Each angler spent an average of $518 on trip-related costs during 2006.

Anglers spent $222 million on equipment in Alabama in 2006, 32 percent of all fishing expenditures. Fishing equipment (rods, reels, line, etc.) spending totaled $140 million—63 percent of the equipment total. Auxiliary equipment expenditures (tents, special fishing clothes, etc.) and special equipment expenditures (boats, vans, etc.) amounted to $82 million—37 percent of the equipment total. Special and auxiliary equipment are items that were purchased for fishing but could be used in activities other than fishing.

The purchase of other items, such as magazines, membership dues, licenses, permits, stamps, and land leasing and ownership, amounted to $60 million—9 percent of all fishing expenditures. For more details about fishing expenditures in Alabama, see Tables 19 and 21 through 23.

Fishing Expenditures in Alabama
(State residents and nonresidents 16 years old and older)

Total	**$700 million**
Trip-related	$417 million
Equipment	$222 million
Fishing	$140 million
Auxiliary and special	$82 million
Other	$60 million

Source: Table 19.

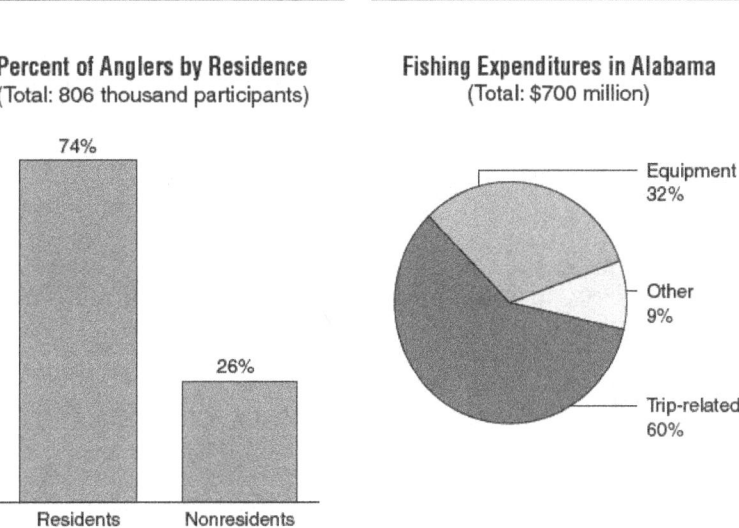

Percent of Anglers by Residence
(Total: 806 thousand participants)

74% Residents
26% Nonresidents

Fishing Expenditures in Alabama
(Total: $700 million)

Equipment 32%
Other 9%
Trip-related 60%

Hunters

Participants and Days of Hunting

In 2006, there were 391 thousand residents and nonresidents 16 years old and older who hunted in Alabama. Resident hunters numbered 310 thousand, accounting for 79 percent of the hunters in Alabama. There were 81 thousand nonresidents who hunted in Alabama—21 percent of the State's hunters. Residents and nonresidents hunted 8.6 million days in 2006, an average of 22 days per hunter. Residents hunted 7.6 million days in Alabama or 88 percent of all hunting days, while nonresidents spent 1 million days hunting in Alabama or 12 percent of all hunting days.

There were 312 thousand Alabama residents 16 years old and older who hunted in the United States in 2006 for a total of 8.0 million days. An estimated 99 percent of all Alabama residents who hunted did so in their home state. Of all hunting days by Alabama residents, 95 percent or 7.6 million were spent pursuing game in their home state.

Some state residents hunted in states other than Alabama. Altogether, 40 thousand or 13 percent of all Alabama hunters hunted in other states. Their 427 thousand days of hunting in other states represented 5 percent of all days Alabama residents spent hunting in 2006. For more information on hunting activities by Alabama residents, see Table 3.

Hunters in Alabama
(State residents and nonresidents 16 years old and older)

Hunters.	**391 thousand**
Resident	310 thousand
Nonresident	81 thousand
Days of hunting	**8.6 million**
Resident	7.6 million
Nonresident	1.0 million

Source: Table 3.

In State/Out of State
(State residents 16 years old and older)

Alabama hunters.	**312 thousand**
In Alabama	310 thousand
In other states.	40 thousand
Days of hunting	**8.0 million**
In Alabama	7.6 million
In other states.	427 thousand

Note: Detail does not add to total because of multiple responses.

Source: Table 3.

Hunting Expenditures in Alabama

All hunting-related expenditures in Alabama totaled $678 million in 2006. Trip-related expenses, such as food and lodging, transportation, and other trip expenses, totaled $239 million—35 percent of total expenditures. Expenditures for food and lodging were $83 million and transportation expenditures were $85 million. Other trip expenses, such as equipment rental, totaled $72 million for the year. The average trip-related expenditure per hunter was $612.

Hunters spent $316 million on equipment—47 percent of all hunting expenditures. Hunting equipment (guns, ammunition, etc.) totaled $151 million and made up 48 percent of all equipment costs. Hunters spent $165 million on auxiliary equipment (tents, special hunting clothes, etc.) and special equipment (boats, vans, etc.), accounting for 52 percent of total equipment expenditures for hunting. Special and auxiliary equipment are items that were purchased for hunting but could be used in activities other than hunting.

The purchase of other items, such as magazines, membership dues, licenses, permits, and land leasing and ownership, cost hunters $123 million—18 percent of all hunting expenditures. For more details on hunting expenditures in Alabama, see Tables 20 through 23.

Hunting Expenditures in Alabama
(State residents and nonresidents 16 years old and older)

Total	**$678 million**
Trip-related	$239 million
Equipment	$316 million
Hunting	$151 million
Auxiliary and special	$165 million
Other	$123 million

Source: Table 20.

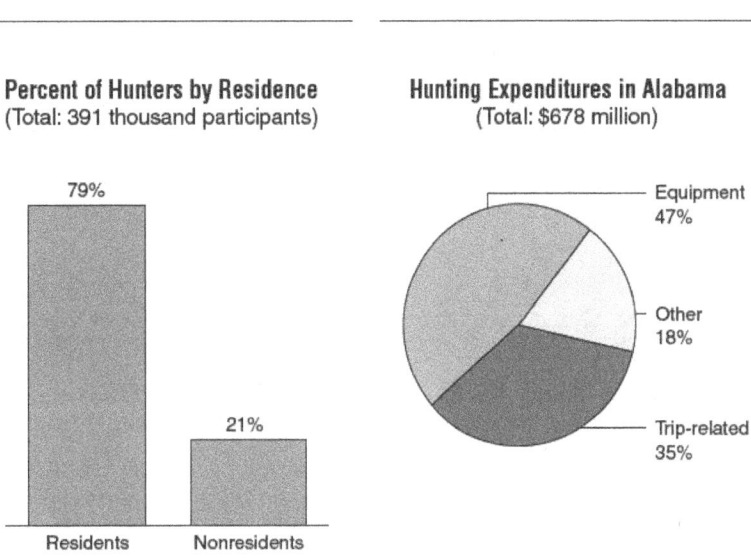

Percent of Hunters by Residence
(Total: 391 thousand participants)

Residents 79%
Nonresidents 21%

Hunting Expenditures in Alabama
(Total: $678 million)

Equipment 47%
Other 18%
Trip-related 35%

Wildlife Watchers

Participants and Days of Activity

In 2006, 1.2 million U.S. residents 16 years old and older fed, observed, or photographed wildlife in Alabama.

Most of them, 85 percent (989 thousand), enjoyed their activities close to home and are called "around-the-home" participants. Those persons who enjoyed wildlife at least 1 mile from home are called "away-from-home" participants. People participating in away-from-home activities in Alabama in 2006 numbered 471 thousand—41 percent of all wildlife watchers in Alabama. Of the 471 thousand, 315 thousand were state residents and 156 thousand were nonresidents.

Alabamians 16 years old and older who enjoyed away-from-home wildlife watching within their state totaled 315 thousand. Of this group, 290 thousand participants observed wildlife, 144 thousand fed wildlife, and 133 thousand photographed wildlife. Since some individuals engaged in more than 1 of the 3 away-from-home activities during the year, the sum of wildlife observers, feeders, and photographers exceeds the total number of away-from-home participants.

Alabamians spent nearly 3.4 million days engaged in away-from-home wildlife-watching activities in their state. They spent 2.3 million days observing wildlife, 1.5 million days feeding wildlife, and 644 thousand days photographing wildlife. The sum of days observing, feeding, and photographing wildlife exceeds the total days of wildlife-watching activity because individuals may have engaged in more than one activity on some days. For further details about away-from-home activities, see Table 25.

Alabama residents also took an active interest in wildlife around their homes. In 2006, 989 thousand state residents enjoyed observing, feeding, and photographing wildlife within 1 mile of their homes. Among this around-the-home group, 924 thousand fed, 676 thousand observed, and 258 thousand photographed wildlife around their homes. Another 167 thousand participants maintained natural areas of ¼ acre or more for wildlife; 96 thousand participants maintained plantings for the benefit of wildlife; and 115 thousand

---

Wildlife-Watching Participants in Alabama
(State residents and nonresidents 16 years old and older)

Total	**1.2 million**
Around the home	989 thousand
Away from home	471 thousand

Note: Detail does not add to total because of multiple responses.

Source Table 24.

Away-From-Home Wildlife-Watching Participation in Alabama
(State residents and nonresidents 16 years old and older)

Participants, total	**471 thousand**
Observe wildlife	445 thousand
Feed wildlife	181 thousand
Photograph wildlife	257 thousand
Days, total	**4.0 million**
Observe wildlife	2.8 million
Feed wildlife	1.8 million
Photograph wildlife	1.0 million

Note: Detail does not add to total because of multiple responses.

Source Table 25.

Around-the-Home Wildlife-Watching Participation in Alabama
(State residents 16 years old and older)

Total	**989 thousand**
Feed wildlife	924 thousand
Observe wildlife	676 thousand
Photograph wildlife	258 thousand
Maintain natural areas	167 thousand
Maintain plantings	96 thousand
Visit public areas	115 thousand

Note: Detail does not add to total because of multiple responses.

Source Table 27.

participants visited public parks within a mile of home because of the wildlife. Summing the number of participants in these six activities results in an estimate that exceeds the total number of around-the-home participants because many people participated in more than one type of around-the-home activity. In addition, 33 percent of Alabamian around-the-home wildlife watchers also enjoyed wildlife away from home. For further details about Alabama residents participating in around-the-home wildlife-watching activities, see Table 27.

Wild Bird Observers

Bird watching attracted many wildlife enthusiasts in Alabama. In 2006, 828 thousand people observed birds around the home and on trips in the state. A majority, 76 percent (633 thousand), observed wild birds around the home

while 49 percent (404 thousand) took trips away from home to watch birds.

Wildlife-Watching Expenditures in Alabama

Wildlife watchers spent $450 million on wildlife-watching activities in Alabama in 2006. Trip-related expenditures, including food and lodging ($78 million), transportation ($47 million), and other trip expenses ($27 million), such as equipment rental, amounted to nearly $152 million. This summation comprised 34 percent of all wildlife-watching expenditures by participants. The average of the trip-related expenditures for away-from-home participants was $309 per person in 2006.

Wildlife-watching participants spent nearly $259 million on equipment—57 percent of all their expenditures. Specifically, wildlife-watching equip-

ment (binoculars, special clothing, etc.) expenditures totaled $138 million, 53 percent of the equipment total. Auxiliary equipment expenditures (tents, backpacking equipment, etc.) and special equipment expenditures (campers, trucks, etc.) amounted to $121 million—47 percent of all equipment costs. Special and auxiliary equipment are items that were purchased for wildlife-watching recreation but can be used in activities other than wildlife-watching activities.

Other items purchased by wildlife-watching participants, such as magazines, membership dues and contributions, land leasing and ownership, and plantings, totaled $40 million—9 percent of all wildlife-watching expenditures. For more details about wildlife-watching expenditures in Alabama, see Table 31.

Wild Bird Observers in Alabama
(State residents and nonresidents 16 years old and older)

Participants, total	**828 thousand**
Around the home	633 thousand
Away from home	404 thousand
Days, total	**85.6 million**
Around the home	82.5 million
Away from home	3.1 million

Note: Detail does not add to total because of multiple responses.

Source Table 29.

Wildlife-Watching Expenditures in Alabama
(State residents and nonresidents 16 years old and older)

Total	**$450 million**
Trip-related	$152 million
Equipment	$259 million
Wildlife watching	$138 million
Auxiliary and special	$121 million
Other	$40 million

Source: Table 31.

Around-the-Home and Away-From-Home Participation by Alabama Residents
(Total: 989 thousand participants)

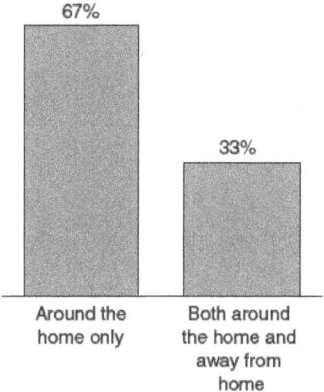

Wildlife-Watching Expenditures in Alabama
(Total: $450 million)

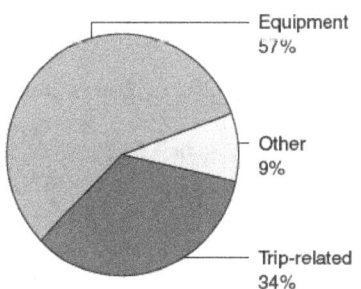

1996–2006 Comparisons

Comparing the estimates from the 1996, 2001, and 2006 Surveys gives a perspective on the state of wildlife-related recreation in the late 1990s and early-to-mid 2000s in Alabama. Only the most general recreation comparisons are presented here.

The best way to compare estimates from surveys is not to compare the estimates themselves but to compare the confidence intervals around the estimates. A 90-percent confidence interval around an estimate gives the range of estimates that 90 percent of all possible representative samples would supply. If the 90-percent confidence intervals of two surveys' estimates overlap, it is not possible to say the two estimates are statistically different.

The state resident estimates cover the participation and expenditure activity of Alabama residents anywhere in the United States. The in-state estimates cover the participation, day, and expenditure activity of U.S. residents in Alabama.

The expenditure estimates were made comparable by adjusting the estimates for inflation—all estimates are in 2006 dollars.

Alabama 1996 and 2006 Comparison
(Numbers in thousands)

	1996	2006	Percent change
Fishing			
Anglers in state	984	806	*
Days in state	16,553	13,708	*
In-state expenditures by U.S. anglers	$1,077,945	$699,532	*
State resident anglers	698	628	*
Total expenditures by state residents	$970,930	$791,187	*
Hunting			
Hunters in state	347	391	*
Days in state	7,181	8,649	*
In-state expenditures by U.S. hunters	$787,299	$678,024	*
State resident hunters	265	312	*
Total expenditures by state residents	$684,735	$596,485	*
Away-From-Home Wildlife Watching			
Participants in state	336	471	*
Days in state	3,105	4,023	*
State resident participants	259	348	*
Around-the-Home Wildlife Watching			
Total participants	970	989	*
Observers	633	676	*
Feeders	924	924	*
Wildlife-Watching Expenditures			
In-state expenditures by U.S. wildlife watchers	$359,838	$450,004	*
Total expenditures by state residents	$356,423	$493,849	*

*Not different from zero at the 10 percent level of significance.

Alabama 2001 and 2006 Comparison
(Numbers in thousands)

	2001	2006	Percent change
Fishing			
Anglers in state	851	806	*
Days in state	11,275	13,708	*
In-state expenditures by U.S. anglers	$824,752	$699,532	*
State resident anglers	634	628	*
Total expenditures by state residents	$684,415	$791,187	*
Hunting			
Hunters in state	423	391	*
Days in state	7,616	8,649	*
In-state expenditures by U.S. hunters	$756,477	$678,024	*
State resident hunters	316	312	*
Total expenditures by state residents	$744,243	$596,485	*
Away-From-Home Wildlife Watching			
Participants in state	276	471	71
Days in state	3,643	4,023	*
State resident participants	280	348	*
Around-the-Home Wildlife Watching			
Total participants...................................	925	989	*
Observers	634	676	*
Feeders	835	924	*
Wildlife-Watching Expenditures			
In-state expenditures by U.S. wildlife watchers	$714,096	$450,004	*
Total expenditures by state residents	$755,334	$493,849	*

*Not different from zero at the 10 percent level of significance.

Number of People Who Hunted and Fished in Alabama: 1996–2006
(In thousands)

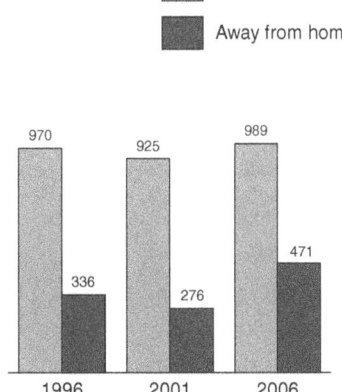

Number of People Who Wildlife Watched in Alabama: 1996–2006
(In thousands)

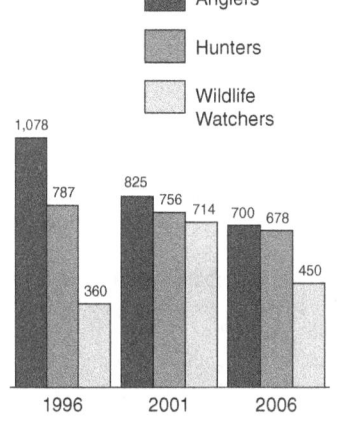

Total Expenditures by Participants in Alabama
(In millions of 2006 dollars)

Guide to Statistical Tables

Purpose and Coverage of Tables

The statistical tables of this report were designed to meet a wide range of needs for those interested in wildlife-related recreation. Special terms used in these tables are defined in Appendix A.

The tables are based on responses to the 2006 Survey, which was designed to collect data about participation in wildlife-related recreation. To have taken part in the Survey, a respondent must have been a U.S. resident (a resident of one of the 50 states or the District of Columbia). No one residing outside the United States (including U.S. citizens) was eligible for interviewing. Therefore, reported state and national totals do not include participation by those who were not U.S. residents or who were U.S. citizens residing outside the United States.

Comparability With Previous Surveys

The numbers reported can be compared with those in the 1991, 1996, and 2001 Survey Reports. The methodology used in 2006 was similar to that used in those Surveys. These results should not be directly compared to results from Surveys earlier than 1991 since there were major changes in methodology in 1991. These changes were made to improve accuracy in the estimates.

Coverage of an Individual Table

Since the Survey covers many activities in various places by participants of different ages, all table titles, headnotes, stubs, and footnotes are designed to identify and articulate each item being reported in the table. For example, the title of Table 2 shows that data about anglers and hunters, their days of participation, and their number of trips are reported by type of activity. By contrast, the title of Table 7 indicates that it contains data on freshwater anglers and the days they fished for different species.

Percentages Reported in the Tables

Percentages are reported in the tables for the convenience of the user. When exclusive groups are being reported, the base of a percentage is apparent from its context because the percents add to 100 percent (plus or minus a rounding error). For example, Table 2 reports the number of trips taken by big game hunters, those taken by small game hunters, those taken by migratory bird hunters, and those taken by hunters pursuing other animals. These comprise 100 percent because they are exclusive categories.

Percents should not add to 100 when nonexclusive groups are being reported. Using Table 2 as an example again, note that adding the percentages associated with the total number of big game hunters, total small game hunters, total migratory bird hunters, and total hunters of other animals will not yield total hunters because respondents could hunt for more than one type of game.

When the base of the percentage is not apparent in context, it is identified in a footnote. For example, Table 15 reports two percentages with different bases: one base being the number of total participants at the head of the column and the other base being the total population who are described by the row category. Footnotes are used to clarify the bases of the reported percentages.

Footnotes to the Tables

Footnotes are used to clarify the information or items that are being reported in a table. Symbols in the body of a table indicate important footnotes. These symbols are used in the tables to refer to the same footnote each time they appear:

* Estimate based on a sample size of 10–29.

... Sample size too small to report data reliably because there were fewer than 10 responses.

W Less than .5 dollars.

Z Less than 0.5 percent.

X Not applicable.

NA Not asked.

Estimates based upon fewer than 10 responses are regarded as being based on a sample size that is too small for reliable reporting. An estimate based upon at least 10 but fewer than 30 responses is treated as an estimate based on a small sample size. Other footnotes appear, as necessary, to qualify or clarify the estimates reported in the tables. In addition, these two important footnotes appear frequently:

• Detail does not add to total because of multiple responses.

• Detail does not add to total because of multiple responses and nonresponse.

"Multiple responses" is a term used to reflect the fact that individuals or their characteristics fall into more than one category. Using Table 12 as an example, those who hunt for big game, small game, migratory birds, and other animals are counted only once as a hunter in the "Total, all hunting" row. Another example is Table 15, where total anglers and hunters add up to more than total sportspersons. Totals will be smaller than the sum of subcategories when multiple responses exist.

"Nonresponse" exists because the Survey questions were answered voluntarily and some respondents did not or could not answer all the questions. Totals are greater than the sum of subcategories when nonresponses have occurred. This occurs because some respondents answered the question that provided the category estimate but did not answer the subcategory questions.

Table 1. Fishing and Hunting in Alabama by Resident and Nonresident Sportspersons: 2006

(Population 16 years old and older. Numbers in thousands)

Sportspersons	Total, state residents and nonresidents		State residents		Nonresidents	
	Number	Percent of sportspersons	Number	Percent of resident sportspersons	Number	Percent of nonresident sportspersons
Total sportspersons (fished or hunted)	**962**	**100**	**689**	**100**	**273**	**100**
Total anglers	**806**	**84**	**600**	**87**	**206**	**75**
Fished only...........................	571	59	379	55	192	70
Fished and hunted	235	24	221	32	...	...
Total hunters...........................	**391**	**41**	**310**	**45**	**81**	**30**
Hunted only	156	16	89	13	*67	*25
Hunted and fished	235	24	221	32	...	...

* Estimate based on a sample size of 10–29.   ... Sample size too small to report data reliably.

Note: Detail does not add to total because of multiple responses.

Table 2. Anglers and Hunters, Days of Participation, and Trips in Alabama by Type of Fishing and Hunting: 2006

(Population 16 years old and older. Numbers in thousands)

Type of fishing and hunting	Participants		Days of participation		Trips	
	Number	Percent	Number	Percent	Number	Percent
FISHING						
Total, all fishing	**806**	**100**	**13,708**	**100**	**11,331**	**100**
Total, all freshwater......................	714	89	12,987	95	10,713	95
Freshwater, except Great Lakes............	714	89	12,987	95	10,713	95
Great Lakes	...	...	...	...	...	...
Saltwater...............................	153	19	758	6	618	5
HUNTING						
Total, all hunting	**391**	**100**	**8,649**	**100**	**7,804**	**100**
Big game	352	90	7,685	89	6,097	78
Small game...........................	126	32	1,311	15	1,150	15
Migratory bird	73	19	401	5	278	4
Other animals...........................	...	...	...	...	...	...

... Sample size too small to report data reliably.

Note: Detail does not add to total because of multiple responses.

Table 3. Anglers and Hunters, Trips, and Days of Participation: 2006

(Population 16 years old and older. Numbers in thousands)

Anglers and hunters, trips, and days of participation	Activity in Alabama						Activity by Alabama residents in United States					
	Total, state residents and nonresidents		State residents		Nonresidents		Total, in state of residence and in other states		In state of residence		In other states	
	Number	Percent	Number	Percent	Number	Percent	Number	Percent	Number	Percent	Number	Percent
FISHING												
Total anglers	806	100	600	74	206	26	628	100	600	96	107	17
Total trips	11,331	100	10,757	95	574	5	11,169	100	10,757	96	412	4
Total days of fishing.	13,708	100	12,686	93	1,022	7	13,164	100	12,686	96	600	5
Average days of fishing	17	(X)	21	(X)	5	(X)	21	(X)	21	(X)	6	(X)
HUNTING												
Total hunters	391	100	310	79	81	21	312	100	310	99	*40	*13
Total trips	7,804	100	7,291	93	513	7	7,503	100	7,291	97	*212	*3
Total days of hunting	8,649	100	7,609	88	1,039	12	8,032	100	7,609	95	*427	*5
Average days of hunting	22	(X)	25	(X)	13	(X)	26	(X)	25	(X)	*11	(X)

(X) Not applicable.   * Estimate based on a sample size of 10–29.

Note: Detail does not add to total because of multiple responses.

Table 4. Alabama Resident Anglers and Hunters by Place Fished or Hunted: 2006

(State population 16 years old and older. Numbers in thousands)

Place fished or hunted	Anglers		Hunters	
	Number	Percent	Number	Percent
Total, all places.	**628**	**100**	**312**	**100**
In-state only.	521	83	272	87
In-state and other states.	79	13	*37	*12
In other states only	*28	*4	...	...

* Estimate based on a sample size of 10–29.   ... Sample size too small to report data reliably.

Note: Detail may not add to total because of multiple responses and nonresponse.

Table 5. Alabama Resident Anglers and Hunters, Days of Participation, and Trips in the United States by Type of Fishing and Hunting: 2006

(State population 16 years old and older. Numbers in thousands)

Type of fishing and hunting	Participants		Days of participation		Trips	
	Number	Percent	Number	Percent	Number	Percent
FISHING						
Total, all fishing	**628**	**100**	**13,164**	**100**	**11,169**	**100**
Total, all freshwater.......................	579	92	12,540	95	10,548	94
Freshwater, except Great Lakes............	579	92	12,540	95	10,540	94
Great Lakes	...	...	...	...	...	...
Saltwater...............................	134	21	757	6	621	6
HUNTING						
Total, all hunting	**312**	**100**	**8,032**	**100**	**7,503**	**100**
Big game	288	92	7,251	90	5,918	79
Small game.............................	102	33	1,062	13	1,008	13
Migratory bird	64	20	425	5	300	4
Other animals...........................	...	...	...	...	...	...

... Sample size too small to report data reliably.

Note: Detail does not add to total because of multiple responses.

Table 6. Freshwater Anglers, Trips, Days of Fishing, and Type of Water Fished: 2006

(Population 16 years old and older. Numbers in thousands)

Anglers, trips, and days of fishing	Activity in Alabama					
	Total, state residents and nonresidents		State residents		Nonresidents	
	Number	Percent	Number	Percent	Number	Percent
Total anglers...........................	**714**	**100**	**567**	**79**	**147**	**21**
Total trips..............................	**10,713**	**100**	**10,288**	**96**	**425**	**4**
Total days of fishing......................	**12,987**	**100**	**12,202**	**94**	**785**	**6**
Average days of fishing.....................	18	(X)	22	(X)	5	(X)
ANGLERS						
Total, all types of water...................	**714**	**100**	**567**	**79**	**147**	**21**
Ponds, lakes or reservoirs	518	100	405	78	113	22
Rivers or streams........................	436	100	380	87	*56	*13
DAYS						
Total, all types of water...................	**12,987**	**100**	**12,202**	**94**	**785**	**6**
Ponds, lakes or reservoirs	6,939	100	6,316	91	623	9
Rivers or streams........................	8,020	100	7,816	97	*205	*3

* Estimate based on a sample size of 10–29.   (X) Not applicable.

Note: Detail does not add to total because of multiple responses.

Table 7. Freshwater Anglers and Days of Fishing in Alabama by Type of Fish: 2006

(Population 16 years old and older. Numbers in thousands)

Anglers and days of fishing	Activity in Alabama						
	Total, state residents and nonresidents			State residents		Nonresidents	
	Number	Percent of total types	Percent of anglers/ days	Number	Percent of anglers/ days	Number	Percent of anglers/ days
ANGLERS							
Total, all types of fish	**714**	**100**	**100**	**567**	**79**	**147**	**21**
Crappie....................................	295	41	100	252	86	*43	*14
Panfish	150	21	100	115	77	*35	*23
White bass, striped bass, striped bass hybrids	191	27	100	149	78	*42	*22
Black bass	399	56	100	312	78	*87	*22
Catfish, bullheads............................	245	34	100	229	94	...	...
Walleye, sauger	...	...	...	...	...	...	...
Northern pike, pickerel, muskie, muskie hybrids...	...	...	...	...	...	...	...
Steelhead	...	...	...	...	...	...	...
Trout......................................	...	...	...	...	...	...	...
Salmon	...	...	...	...	...	...	...
Anything[1].................................	115	16	100	105	91	...	...
Other freshwater fish........................	*66	*9	*100	*52	*78	...	...
DAYS							
Total, all types of fish	**12,987**	**100**	**100**	**12,202**	**94**	**785**	**6**
Crappie....................................	4,184	32	100	4,010	96	*174	*4
Panfish	1,949	15	100	1,803	93	*145	*7
White bass, striped bass, striped bass hybrids	2,938	23	100	2,658	90	*280	*10
Black bass	8,371	64	100	7,836	94	*536	*6
Catfish, bullheads............................	3,962	31	100	3,878	98	...	...
Walleye, sauger	...	...	...	...	...	...	...
Northern pike, pickerel, muskie, muskie hybrids...	...	...	...	...	...	...	...
Steelhead	...	...	...	...	...	...	...
Trout......................................	...	...	...	...	...	...	...
Salmon	...	...	...	...	...	...	...
Anything[1].................................	869	7	100	848	98	...	...
Other freshwater fish........................	*763	*6	*100	*746	*98	...	...

* Estimate based on a sample size of 10–29.   ... Sample size too small to report data reliably.

[1] Respondent fished for no specific species and identified "Anything" from a list of categories of fish.

Note: Detail does not add to total because of multiple responses.

Table 8. Great Lakes Anglers, Trips, and Days of Fishing in Alabama: 2006

This table does not apply to this state.

Table 9. Great Lakes Anglers and Days of Fishing in Alabama by Type of Fish: 2006

This table does not apply to this state.

(Population 16 years old and older. Numbers in thousands)

Anglers, trips, and days of fishing	Activity in Alabama					
	Total, state residents and nonresidents		State residents		Nonresidents	
	Number	Percent	Number	Percent	Number	Percent
Total anglers.............................	153	100	89	59	*63	*41
Total trips...............................	618	100	469	76	*149	*24
Total days...............................	758	100	530	70	*229	*30
Average days of fishing.....................	5	(X)	6	(X)	*4	(X)

* Estimate based on a sample size of 10–29.　　... Sample size too small to report data reliably.　　(X) Not applicable.

Note: Detail does not add to total because of multiple responses.

Table 11. Saltwater Anglers and Days of Fishing in Alabama by Type of Fish: 2006

(Population 16 years old and older. Numbers in thousands)

Anglers and days of fishing	Activity in Alabama					
	Total, state residents and nonresidents			State residents		Nonresidents	
	Number	Percent of total types	Percent of anglers/ days	Number	Percent of anglers/ days	Number	Percent of anglers/ days
ANGLERS							
Total, all types of fish	**153**	**100**	**100**	**89**	**59**	***63**	***41**
Salmon............................	...	...	...	...	...	...	...
Striped bass	...	...	...	...	...	...	...
Bluefish	...	...	...	...	...	...	...
Flatfish (flounder, halibut).............	*47	*31	*100	*27	*58	...	...
Red drum (redfish)	*64	*42	*100	*27	*41	*38	*59
Sea trout (weakfish)...................	*35	*23	*100	...	...	...	...
Mackerel...........................	...	...	...	...	...	...	...
Mahi-mahi	...	...	...	...	...	...	...
Shellfish	...	...	...	...	...	...	...
Anything[1]...........................	*61	*40	*100	*30	*50	...	...
Other saltwater fish...................	*48	*32	*100	*25	*52	...	...
DAYS							
Total, all types of fish	**758**	**100**	**100**	**530**	**70**	***229**	***30**
Salmon............................	...	...	...	...	...	...	...
Striped bass	...	...	...	...	...	...	...
Bluefish	...	...	...	...	...	...	...
Flatfish (flounder, halibut).............	*268	*35	*100	*202	*75	...	...
Red drum (redfish)	*304	*40	*100	*194	*64	*110	*36
Sea trout (weakfish)..................	*132	*17	*100	...	...	...	...
Mackerel...........................	...	...	...	...	...	...	...
Mahi-mahi	...	...	...	...	...	...	...
Shellfish	...	...	...	...	...	...	...
Anything[1]...........................	*273	*36	*100	*178	*65	...	...
Other saltwater fish...................	*214	*28	*100	*152	*71	...	...

* Estimate based on a sample size of 10–29.　　... Sample size too small to report data reliably.

[1] Respondent fished for no specific species and identified "Anything" from a list of categories of fish.

Note: Detail does not add to total because of multiple responses.

Table 12. **Hunters, Trips, and Days of Hunting in Alabama by Type of Hunting: 2006**

(Population 16 years old and older. Numbers in thousands)

Hunters, trips, and days of hunting	Activity in Alabama					
	Total, state residents and nonresidents		State residents		Nonresidents	
	Number	Percent	Number	Percent	Number	Percent
HUNTERS						
Total, all hunting	**391**	**100**	**310**	**79**	**81**	**21**
Big game	352	100	282	80	*70	*20
Small game............................	126	100	102	81	...	...
Migratory bird	73	100	62	85	...	...
Other animals...........................	...	...	...	...	...	...
TRIPS						
Total, all hunting	**7,804**	**100**	**7,291**	**93**	**513**	**7**
Big game	6,097	100	5,757	94	*340	*6
Small game............................	1,150	100	998	87	...	...
Migratory bird	278	100	260	93	...	...
Other animals...........................	...	...	...	...	...	...
DAYS						
Total, all hunting	**8,649**	**100**	**7,609**	**88**	**1,039**	**12**
Big game	7,685	100	6,928	90	*757	*10
Small game............................	1,311	100	1,050	80	...	...
Migratory bird	401	100	337	84	...	...
Other animals...........................	...	...	...	...	...	...

* Estimate based on a sample size of 10–29.   ... Sample size too small to report data reliably.

Note: Detail does not add to total because of multiple responses.

Table 10. **Hunters and Days of Hunting in Alabama by Type of Game: 2006**

(Population 16 years old and older. Numbers in thousands)

Type of game	Hunters, state residents and nonresidents		Days of hunting	
	Number	Percent	Number	Percent
Total, all types of game	**391**	**100**	**8,649**	**100**
Big game, total	**352**	**90**	**7,685**	**89**
Deer	334	86	6,860	79
Elk	...	...	...	...
Bear	...	...	...	...
Wild turkey....................................	98	25	1,482	17
Other big game	...	...	...	...
Small game, total	**126**	**32**	**1,311**	**15**
Rabbit, hare	*66	*17	*671	*8
Quail..	*31	*8	*159	*2
Grouse/prairie chicken.........................	...	...	...	...
Squirrel.......................................	86	22	834	10
Pheasant	...	...	...	...
Other small game...............................	...	...	...	...
Migratory birds, total	**73**	**19**	**401**	**5**
Waterfowl......................................	*24	*6	*162	*2
Geese	...	...	...	...
Duck...	*24	*6	*157	*2
Dove...	*59	*15	*215	*2
Other migratory bird	...	...	...	...
Other animals, total [1]	...	...	...	...

* Estimate based on a sample size of 10–29.   ... Sample size too small to report data reliably.

[1] Includes groundhog, raccoon, fox, coyote, crow, prairie dog, etc.

Note: Detail does not add to total because of multiple responses.

Table 14. **Hunters and Days of Hunting in Alabama by Type of Land: 2006**

(Population 16 years old and older. Numbers in thousands)

Hunters and days of hunting	Total, state residents and nonresidents		State residents		Nonresidents	
	Number	Percent	Number	Percent	Number	Percent
HUNTERS						
Total, all types of land.......................	391	100	310	100	81	100
Public land, total	**95**	**24**	**86**	**28**	...	...
Public land only........................	*26	*7	...	...	...	...
Public and private land	69	18	67	22	...	...
Private land, total........................	**355**	**91**	**286**	**92**	***69**	***85**
Private land only	286	73	219	71	*67	*83
Private and public land	69	18	67	22	...	...
DAYS						
Total, all types of land.......................	8,649	100	7,609	100	1,039	100
Public land[1]	1,276	15	1,207	16	...	...
Private land[2]............................	7,905	91	7,029	92	*877	*84

* Estimate based on a sample size of 10–29.   ... Sample size too small to report data reliably.

[1] Days of hunting on public land includes both days spent solely on public land and those spent on public and private land.
[2] Days of hunting on private land includes both days spent solely on private land and those spent on private and public land.

Note: Detail does not add to total because of multiple responses and nonresponse.

Table 15. **Selected Characteristics of Alabama Resident Anglers and Hunters: 2006**

(State population 16 years old and older. Numbers in thousands)

Characteristic	Population		Sportspersons (fished or hunted)			Anglers			Hunters		
	Number	Percent	Number	Percent who partici-pated	Percent of sports-persons	Number	Percent who partici-pated	Percent of anglers	Number	Percent who partici-pated	Percent of hunters
Total persons....................	**3,550**	**100**	**707**	**20**	**100**	**628**	**18**	**100**	**312**	**9**	**100**
Population Density of Residence											
Urban	1,931	54	297	15	42	269	14	43	91	5	29
Rural........................	1,620	46	410	25	58	358	22	57	221	14	71
Population Size of Residence											
Metropolitan statistical area											
(MSA).......................	2,598	73	530	20	75	472	18	75	221	9	71
1,000,000 or more	981	28	210	21	30	190	19	30	90	9	29
250,000 to 999,999	946	27	170	18	24	151	16	24	*55	*6	*18
Less than 250,000	671	19	150	22	21	131	19	21	76	11	24
Outside MSA..................	952	27	177	19	25	156	16	25	91	10	29
Sex											
Male	1,658	47	544	33	77	467	28	74	278	17	89
Female	1,892	53	163	9	23	160	8	26	*34	*2	*11
Age											
16 to 17 years	137	4	*47	*34	*7	*42	*31	*7	...	...	...
18 to 24 years	307	9	*57	*19	*8	*57	*19	*9	*35	*11	*11
25 to 34 years	513	14	111	22	16	99	19	16	*41	*8	*13
35 to 44 years	592	17	139	24	20	115	19	18	74	13	24
45 to 54 years	806	23	166	21	23	150	19	24	75	9	24
55 to 64 years	531	15	97	18	14	81	15	13	*40	*8	*13
65 years and older..............	664	19	89	13	13	83	12	13	*29	*4	*9
Ethnicity											
Hispanic......................	66	2	...	...	...	...	...	...	...	...	...
Non-Hispanic..................	3,485	98	697	20	99	618	18	98	308	9	99
Race											
White	2,649	75	625	24	88	554	21	88	295	11	95
Black........................	845	24	70	8	10	*61	*7	*10	...	...	...
All others	*57	*2	...	...	...	...	...	...	...	...	...
Annual Household Income											
Under $10,000	259	7	*27	*10	*4	*27	*10	*4	...	...	...
$10,000 to $19,999	304	9	*31	*10	*4	*31	*10	*5	...	...	...
$20,000 to $29,999	454	13	107	24	15	98	21	16	*44	*10	*14
$30,000 to $39,999	376	11	111	29	16	104	28	17	*54	*14	*17
$40,000 to $49,999	350	10	91	26	13	73	21	12	*53	*15	*17
$50,000 to $74,999	511	14	120	23	17	105	20	17	*59	*12	*19
$75,000 to $99,999	251	7	*58	*23	*8	*52	*21	*8	*17	*7	*5
$100,000 or more...............	292	8	87	30	12	73	25	12	*42	*14	*13
Not reported...................	753	21	75	10	11	65	9	10	*34	*5	*11
Education											
11 years or less	775	22	149	19	21	133	17	21	*61	*8	*20
12 years	1,238	35	293	24	41	270	22	43	130	10	42
1 to 3 years college	865	24	170	20	24	142	16	23	78	9	25
4 years college or more..........	672	19	95	14	13	83	12	13	*43	*6	*14

* Estimate based on a sample size of 10–29.   ... Sample size too small to report data reliably.

Note: Detail does not add to total because of multiple responses. Percent who participated shows the percent of each row's population who participated in the activity named by the column (the percent of those living in urban areas who fished, etc.). Remaining percent columns show the percent of each column's participants who are described by the row heading (the percent of anglers who lived in urban areas, etc.).

(Population 16 years old and older)

Expenditure item	Amount (thousands of dollars)	Spenders (thousands)	Average per spender (dollars)	Average per sportsperson (dollars)
FISHING AND HUNTING				
Total..	**1,738,540**	**937**	**1,856**	**1,801**
Food and lodging......................................	208,940	739	283	217
Transportation...	186,191	727	256	194
Other trip costs[1]....................................	261,547	636	412	272
Equipment (fishing, hunting).........................	293,251	545	538	302
Auxiliary equipment[2]................................	73,097	210	347	76
Special equipment[3]..................................	524,225	85	6,180	544
Magazines and books..................................	7,346	162	45	7
Membership dues and contributions	17,698	91	194	17
Other[4]..	166,244	481	346	173
FISHING				
Total..	**699,532**	**744**	**940**	**864**
Food and lodging......................................	126,363	587	215	157
Transportation...	101,414	549	185	126
Other trip costs[1]....................................	189,502	577	329	235
Fishing equipment	139,540	434	321	172
Auxiliary equipment[2]................................	*11,462	*51	*226	*14
Special equipment[3]..................................	*70,830	*50	*1,420	*87
Magazines and books..................................	*1,665	*38	*44	*2
Membership dues and contributions	*1,026	*28	*37	*1
Other[4]..	57,730	311	186	71
HUNTING				
Total..	**678,024**	**396**	**1,714**	**1,724**
Food and lodging......................................	82,577	303	273	211
Transportation...	84,777	324	261	217
Other trip costs[1]....................................	72,045	123	585	184
Hunting equipment.....................................	151,297	246	616	380
Auxiliary equipment[2]................................	40,510	134	302	103
Special equipment[3]..................................	*124,087	*20	*6,316	*317
Magazines and books..................................	*1,479	*46	*32	*4
Membership dues and contributions	*12,739	*32	*400	*29
Other[4]..	108,514	248	438	278
UNSPECIFIED[5]				
Total..	**358,569**	**158**	**2,264**	**372**

* Estimate based on a sample size of 10–29.

[1] Includes boating costs, equipment rental, guide fees, access fees, heating and cooking fuel, and ice and bait (for fishing only).
[2] Includes tents, special clothing, etc.
[3] Includes boats, campers, 4x4 vehicles, cabins, etc.
[4] Includes land leasing and ownership, licenses, stamps, tags, and permits.
[5] Respondent could not specify whether expenditure was primarily for either fishing or hunting.

Note: Detail does not add to total because of multiple responses and nonresponse. See Tables 19–20 for a detailed listing of expenditure items.

Table 17. Summary of Fishing Trip and Equipment Expenditures in Alabama by State Residents and Nonresidents Combined by Type of Fishing: 2006

(Population 16 years old and older)

Expenditure item	Amount (thousands of dollars)	Spenders (thousands)	Average per spender (dollars)	Average per angler (dollars)
ALL FISHING				
Total......................	**639,111**	**695**	**920**	**791**
Food and lodging............	126,363	587	215	157
Transportation...............	101,414	549	185	126
Other trip costs..............	189,502	577	329	235
Equipment	221,832	446	497	273
ALL FRESHWATER				
Total......................	**492,788**	**622**	**792**	**688**
Food and lodging............	72,922	530	138	102
Transportation...............	84,152	493	171	118
Other trip costs..............	140,040	516	271	196
Equipment	195,674	389	503	272
FRESHWATER, EXCEPT GREAT LAKES				
Total......................	**492,746**	**621**	**794**	**688**
Food and lodging............	72,922	530	138	102
Transportation...............	84,152	493	171	118
Other trip costs..............	140,040	516	271	196
Equipment	195,632	387	505	272
GREAT LAKES				
Total......................	...	...	...	...
Food and lodging............	...	...	...	...
Transportation...............	...	...	...	...
Other trip costs..............	...	...	...	...
Equipment	...	...	...	...
SALTWATER				
Total......................	**131,290**	**132**	**992**	**856**
Food and lodging............	53,441	107	501	350
Transportation...............	17,262	98	176	113
Other trip costs..............	49,462	108	456	324
Equipment	*11,125	*55	*201	*68

* Estimate based on a sample size of 10–29.   ... Sample size too small to report data reliably.

Note: Detail does not add to total because of multiple responses and nonresponse. See Table 19 for detailed listing of expenditure items.

Table 18. Summary of Hunting Trip and Equipment Expenditures in Alabama by State Residents and Nonresidents Combined by Type of Hunting: 2006

(Population 16 years old and older)

Expenditure item	Amount (thousands of dollars)	Spenders (thousands)	Average per spender (dollars)	Average per hunter (dollars)
ALL HUNTING				
Total..........................	**555,293**	**381**	**1,459**	**1,413**
Food and lodging...............	82,577	303	273	211
Transportation..................	84,777	324	261	217
Other trip costs.................	72,045	123	585	184
Equipment	315,894	266	1,187	800
BIG GAME				
Total..........................	**458,081**	**336**	**1,365**	**1,297**
Food and lodging...............	66,567	270	247	189
Transportation..................	63,588	285	223	181
Other trip costs.................	61,042	111	552	174
Equipment	266,883	224	1,189	753
SMALL GAME				
Total..........................	**50,344**	**106**	**476**	**1,585**
Food and lodging...............	9,302	68	137	395
Transportation..................	16,378	71	230	695
Other trip costs.................	*9,059	*30	*306	*384
Equipment	*15,605	*59	*266	*111
MIGRATORY BIRD				
Total..........................	*18,011	*56	*324	*992
Food and lodging...............	*6,627	*36	*182	*423
Transportation..................	*4,776	*35	*135	*305
Other trip costs.................	...	...	...	...
Equipment	*4,920	*27	*180	*157
OTHER ANIMALS				
Total..........................	...	...	...	...
Food and lodging...............	...	...	...	...
Transportation..................	...	...	...	...
Other trip costs.................	...	...	...	...
Equipment	...	...	...	...

* Estimate based on a sample size of 10–29.   ... Sample size too small to report data reliably.

Note: Detail does not add to total because of multiple responses and nonresponse. See Table 20 for detailed listing of expenditure items.

Table 19. Expenditures in Alabama by State Residents and Nonresidents Combined for Fishing: 2006

(Population 16 years old and older)

Expenditure item	Expenditures Amount (thousands of dollars)	Expenditures Average per angler (dollars)	Spenders Number (thousands)	Spenders Percent of anglers	Spenders Average per spender (dollars)
Total, all items..................................	699,532	864	744	92	940
TRIP-RELATED EXPENDITURES					
Total trip-related.............................	417,279	518	665	82	628
Food and lodging, total	126,363	157	646	80	196
Food	84,271	105	587	73	144
Lodging......................................	42,093	52	79	10	535
Transportation..................................	101,414	126	549	68	185
Other trip costs, total...........................	189,502	235	577	72	329
Privilege and other fees[1]	50,644	63	158	20	320
Boating costs[2]................................	101,870	126	228	28	447
Bait	25,859	32	474	59	55
Ice	8,794	11	349	43	25
Heating and cooking fuel......................	*2,335	*3	*37	*5	*62
EQUIPMENT AND OTHER EXPENDITURES PRIMARILY FOR FISHING					
Fishing equipment, total	139,540	172	434	54	321
Reels, rods, and rod-making components	66,470	82	283	35	235
Lines, hooks, sinkers, etc......................	23,393	29	383	48	61
Artificial lures and flies.......................	29,182	36	296	37	98
Creels, stringers, fish bags, landing nets, and gaff hooks..	1,821	2	80	10	23
Minnow seines, traps, and bait containers..........	2,556	3	113	14	23
Other fishing equipment[3]	16,118	20	138	17	117
Auxiliary equipment[4]	*11,462	*14	*51	*6	*226
Special equipment[5].............................	*70,830	*87	*50	*6	*1,420
Other fishing costs[6]	60,421	74	347	43	174

* Estimate based on a sample size of 10–29.

[1] Includes boat or equipment rental and fees for guides, pack trip (party and charter boats, etc.), public land use, and private land use.
[2] Boat launching, mooring, storage, maintenance, insurance, pumpout fees, and fuel.
[3] Includes electronic fishing devices (depth finders, fish finders, etc.), tackle boxes, ice fishing equipment, and other fishing equipment.
[4] Includes tents, special fishing clothing, etc.
[5] Includes boats, campers, 4x4 vehicles, cabins, etc.
[6] Includes magazines and books, membership dues and contributions, land leasing and ownership, and licenses, stamps, tags, and permits.

Note: Detail does not add to total because of multiple responses and nonresponse. Percent of anglers may be greater than 100 because spenders who did not fish in this state are included.

Table 20. Expenditures in Alabama by State Residents and Nonresidents Combined for Hunting: 2006

(Population 16 years old and older)

Expenditure item	Expenditures		Spenders		
	Amount (thousands of dollars)	Average per hunter (dollars)	Number (thousands)	Percent of hunters	Average per spender (dollars)
Total, all items.................................	678,024	1,724	396	101	1,714
TRIP-RELATED EXPENDITURES					
Total trip-related..............................	239,398	612	355	91	675
Food and lodging, total	82,577	211	352	90	234
Food	71,476	183	303	77	236
Lodging......................................	*11,101	*28	*54	*14	*206
Transportation.................................	84,777	217	324	83	261
Other trip costs, total..........................	72,045	184	123	32	585
Privilege and other fees[1]	64,540	165	95	24	682
Boating costs.................................	...	...	...	...	...
Heating and cooking fuel.......................	...	...	...	...	...
EQUIPMENT AND OTHER EXPENDITURES PRIMARILY FOR HUNTING					
Hunting equipment, total........................	151,297	380	246	63	616
Firearms	79,121	198	99	25	802
Ammunition	17,235	44	202	52	85
Other hunting equipment[2]	54,941	138	144	37	382
Auxiliary equipment[3]	40,510	103	134	34	302
Special equipment[4].............................	*124,087	*317	*20	*5	*6,316
Other hunting costs[5]............................	122,731	311	263	67	467

* Estimate based on a sample size of 10–29.　　... Sample size too small to report data reliably.

[1] Includes guide fees, pack trip or package fees, public and private land use access fees, and rental of equipment such as boats and hunting or camping equipment.
[2] Includes bows, arrows, archery equipment, telescopic sights, decoys and game calls, handloading equipment and components, hunting dogs and associated costs, hunting knives, and other hunting equipment.
[3] Includes tents, special hunting clothing, etc.
[4] Includes boats, campers, 4x4 vehicles, cabins, etc.
[5] Includes magazines and books, membership dues and contributions, land leasing and ownership, and licenses, stamps, and permits.

Note: Detail does not add to total because of multiple responses and nonresponse. Percent of hunters may be greater than 100 percent because spenders who did not hunt in this state are included.

(Population 16 years old and older)

Expenditure item	Amount (thousands of dollars)	Spenders (thousands)	Average per spender (dollars)	Average per sportsperson (dollars)
STATE RESIDENTS AND NONRESIDENTS				
Trip and equipment expenditures for fishing and hunting, total	**1,532,350**	**869**	**1,764**	**1,593**
Trip and equipment expenditures for fishing, total	**639,111**	**695**	**920**	**793**
Food and lodging	126,363	587	215	157
Transportation	101,414	549	185	126
Boating costs[1]	101,870	228	447	126
Other trip costs[2]	87,632	562	156	109
Equipment	221,832	446	497	275
Trip and equipment expenditures for hunting, total	**555,293**	**381**	**1,459**	**1,421**
Food and lodging	82,577	303	273	211
Transportation	84,777	324	261	217
Boating costs[1]	...	...	...	...
Other trip costs[2]	69,965	118	592	179
Equipment	315,894	266	1,187	808
Unspecified equipment[3]	337,946	62	5,476	351
STATE RESIDENTS				
Trip and equipment expenditures for fishing and hunting, total	**1,304,981**	**633**	**2,062**	**1,894**
Trip and equipment expenditures for fishing, total	**512,096**	**531**	**964**	**854**
Food and lodging	64,723	441	147	108
Transportation	73,788	408	181	123
Boating costs[1]	94,897	194	490	158
Other trip costs[2]	60,560	435	139	101
Equipment	218,128	397	549	364
Trip and equipment expenditures for hunting, total	**454,939**	**297**	**1,531**	**1,469**
Food and lodging	52,989	239	222	171
Transportation	59,999	254	236	194
Boating costs[1]	...	...	...	...
Other trip costs[2]	36,186	84	429	117
Equipment	303,685	240	1,268	980
Unspecified equipment[3]	337,946	62	5,476	491
NONRESIDENTS				
Trip and equipment expenditures for fishing and hunting, total	**227,369**	**236**	**963**	**832**
Trip and equipment expenditures for fishing, total	**127,015**	**164**	**775**	**616**
Food and lodging	61,640	146	423	299
Transportation	27,626	141	196	134
Boating costs[1]	*6,974	*34	*204	*34
Other trip costs[2]	27,072	127	213	131
Equipment	*3,704	*49	*76	*18
Trip and equipment expenditures for hunting, total	**100,354**	**83**	**1,203**	**1,238**
Food and lodging	29,588	64	461	365
Transportation	24,778	70	354	306
Boating costs[1]	...	...	...	...
Other trip costs[2]	*33,779	*34	*996	*417
Equipment	*12,209	*27	*461	*151
Unspecified equipment[3]	...	...	...	...

* Estimate based on a sample size of 10–29.   ... Sample size too small to report data reliably.

[1] Includes boat launching, mooring, storage, maintenance, insurance, pumpout fees, and fuel.
[2] Includes equipment rental, guide and access fees, ice and bait for fishing, and heating and cooking oil.
[3] Respondent could not specify whether item was for hunting or fishing.

Note: Detail does not add to total because of multiple responses and nonresponse.

Table 22. Summary of Alabama Residents' Fishing and Hunting Expenditures Both Inside and Outside Alabama: 2006

(State population 16 years old and older)

Expenditure item	Amount (thousands of dollars)	Spenders (thousands)	Average per spender (dollars)	Average per sportsperson (dollars)
FISHING AND HUNTING				
Total...	**1,761,753**	**685**	**2,570**	**2,492**
Food and lodging...................................	170,608	566	301	241
Transportation.....................................	169,959	552	308	240
Other trip costs[1].................................	234,010	505	463	331
Equipment (fishing, hunting).......................	301,001	501	601	426
Auxiliary equipment[2]..............................	69,389	202	344	98
Special equipment[3]................................	607,941	87	7,021	860
Magazines and books................................	6,796	152	45	10
Membership dues and contributions	15,892	75	213	22
Other[4]	186,156	399	466	263
FISHING				
Total...	**791,187**	**585**	**1,353**	**1,261**
Food and lodging...................................	91,562	481	191	146
Transportation.....................................	91,060	447	204	145
Other trip costs[1].................................	177,943	476	374	284
Fishing equipment	142,476	405	352	227
Auxiliary equipment[2]..............................	*11,469	*51	*225	*18
Special equipment[3]................................	*143,455	*49	*2,954	*229
Magazines and books................................	*1,546	*39	*40	*2
Membership dues and contributions	*724	*20	*37	*1
Other[4]	130,952	274	479	209
HUNTING				
Total...	**596,485**	**310**	**1,926**	**1,911**
Food and lodging...................................	79,046	248	318	253
Transportation.....................................	78,899	260	303	253
Other trip costs[1].................................	56,067	98	570	180
Hunting equipment..................................	154,852	236	657	496
Auxiliary equipment[2]..............................	35,779	121	296	115
Special equipment[3]................................	*124,087	*20	*6,316	*398
Magazines and books................................	*1,076	*35	*30	*3
Membership dues and contributions	*11,475	*29	*402	*37
Other[4]	55,205	214	258	177
UNSPECIFIED[5]				
Total...	**370,408**	**162**	**2,288**	**524**

* Estimate based on a sample size of 10–29.

[1] Includes boating costs, equipment rental, guide fees, access fees, heating and cooking fuel, and ice and bait (for fishing only).
[2] Includes tents, special clothing, etc.
[3] Includes boats, campers, 4x4 vehicles, cabins, etc.
[4] Includes land leasing and ownership, licenses, stamps, tags, and permits.
[5] Respondent could not specify whether expenditure was primarily for either fishing or hunting.

Note: Detail does not add to total because of multiple responses and nonresponse. See Tables 19–20 for a detailed listing of expenditure items.

Table 23. In-State and Out-of-State Expenditures by Alabama Residents for Fishing and Hunting: 2006

(State population 16 years old and older)

Expenditure item	Amount (thousands of dollars)	Spenders (thousands)	Average per spender (dollars)	Average per sportsperson (dollars)
IN ALABAMA				
Expenditures for fishing and hunting, total	**1,444,965**	**666**	**2,171**	**2,098**
Trip-related expenditures	445,222	616	723	646
Equipment (fishing and hunting).......................	284,622	479	594	413
Auxiliary equipment[1]	66,769	188	354	97
Special equipment[2].	523,157	82	6,368	759
Other[3]	125,195	439	285	182
Expenditures for fishing, total	**569,992**	**557**	**1,023**	**950**
Trip-related expenditures	293,968	510	576	490
Fishing equipment	137,166	388	353	229
Auxiliary equipment[1]	*11,201	*48	*233	*19
Special equipment[2].	*69,762	*47	*1,477	*116
Other[3]	57,896	271	213	97
Expenditures for hunting, total	**514,386**	**310**	**1,661**	**1,660**
Trip-related expenditures	151,254	282	536	488
Hunting equipment.	145,155	224	647	469
Auxiliary equipment[1]	34,443	115	300	111
Special equipment[2].	*124,087	*20	*6,316	*401
Other[3]	59,447	217	274	192
Unspecified expenditures for fishing and hunting, total[4]	**357,906**	**141**	**2,540**	**520**
OUT OF STATE				
Expenditures for fishing and hunting, total	**318,155**	**158**	**2,015**	**2,372**
Trip-related expenditures	131,914	122	1,085	984
Equipment (fishing and hunting).......................	*16,221	*57	*287	*121
Auxiliary equipment[1]	...	...	...	...
Special equipment[2].	...	...	...	...
Other[3]	83,363	75	1,107	622
Expenditures for fishing, total	**222,726**	**121**	**1,842**	**2,087**
Trip-related expenditures	68,567	93	740	642
Fishing equipment	*5,263	*43	*123	*49
Auxiliary equipment[1]	...	...	...	...
Special equipment[2].	...	...	...	...
Other[3]	*75,039	*50	*1,499	*703
Expenditures for hunting, total	***82,481**	***47**	***1,740**	***2,072**
Trip-related expenditures	*63,347	*40	*1,591	*1,591
Hunting equipment.	*9,663	*21	*471	*243
Auxiliary equipment[1]	...	...	...	...
Special equipment[2].	...	...	...	...
Other[3]	...	...	...	...
Unspecified expenditures for fishing and hunting, total [4]	...	...	...	...

* Estimate based on a sample size of 10–29.   ... Sample size too small to report data reliably.

[1] Includes tents, special hunting or fishing clothing, etc.
[2] Includes boats, campers, 4x4 vehicles, cabins, etc.
[3] Includes magazines, books, membership dues, contributions, land leasing and ownership, stamps, tags, and licenses.
[4] Respondent could not specify whether expenditure was primarily for either fishing or hunting.

Note: Detail does not add to total because of multiple responses and nonresponse.

Table 24. Wildlife Watching in Alabama by State Residents and Nonresidents Combined: 2006

(Population 16 years old and older. Numbers in thousands)

Participants	Number	Percent
Total participants	**1,161**	**100**
Away from home..	471	41
Observe wildlife	445	38
Photograph wildlife..	*257	*22
Feed wildlife	*181	*16
Around the home..	989	85
Observe wildlife	676	58
Photograph wildlife..	258	22
Feed wildlife	924	80
Visit public parks[1]	*115	*10
Maintain plantings or natural areas	*185	*16

* Estimate based on a sample size of 10–29.

[1] Includes visits only to parks or publicly owned areas within 1 mile of home.

Note: Detail does not add to total because of multiple responses.

Table 25. Participants, Trips, and Days of Participation in Away-From-Home Wildlife Watching in Alabama: 2006

(Population 16 years old and older. Numbers in thousands)

Participants, trips, and days of participation	Activity in Alabama					
	Total, state residents and nonresidents		State residents		Nonresidents	
	Number	Percent	Number	Percent	Number	Percent
PARTICIPANTS						
Total participants........................	**471**	**100**	**315**	**100**	***156**	***100**
Observe wildlife..........................	445	95	290	92	*156	*100
Photograph wildlife	*257	*55	*133	*42	*125	*80
Feed wildlife	*181	*38	*144	*46	...	...
TRIPS						
Total trips................................	2,469	100	2,063	100	*406	*100
Average days per trip......................	2	(X)	2	(X)	*2	(X)
DAYS						
Total days	**4,023**	**100**	**3,365**	**100**	***659**	***100**
Observing wildlife	2,804	70	*2,252	*67	*552	*84
Photographing wildlife....................	*1,007	*25	*644	*19	*363	*55
Feeding wildlife..........................	*1,786	*44	*1,514	*45	...	...
Average days per participant...............	9	(X)	11	(X)	*4	(X)
Observing wildlife	6	(X)	*8	(X)	*4	(X)
Photographing wildlife....................	*4	(X)	*5	(X)	*3	(X)
Feeding wildlife..........................	*10	(X)	*11	(X)	...	(X)

* Estimate based on a sample size of 10–29.   ... Sample size too small to report data reliably.   (X) Not applicable.

Note: Detail does not add to total because of multiple responses and nonresponse.

Table 26. **Away-From-Home Wildlife-Watching Participants by Wildlife Observed, Photographed, or Fed in Alabama: 2006**

(Population 16 years old and older. Numbers in thousands)

Wildlife observed, photographed, or fed	Total, state residents and nonresidents		State residents		Nonresidents	
	Number	Percent	Number	Percent	Number	Percent
Total all wildlife	**471**	**100**	**315**	**67**	***156**	***33**
Total birds...	**411**	**100**	**264**	**64**	***148**	***36**
Songbirds (cardinals, robins, warblers, etc.)...........	305	100	*203	*67	*102	*33
Birds of prey (hawks, owls, eagles, etc.)	*214	*100	*144	*67	...	...
Waterfowl (ducks, geese, swan, etc.)	291	100	*216	*74	...	...
Other water birds (shorebirds, herons, cranes, etc.)....	*221	*100	*158	*71	...	...
Other birds (pheasants, turkeys, road runners, etc.)....	*152	*100	*115	*76	...	...
Total land mammals	**323**	**100**	***241**	***74**	***83**	***26**
Large land mammals (bears, bison, etc.)	*255	*100	*196	*77	...	...
Small land mammals (prairie dogs, squirrels, etc.)	267	100	*185	*69	*83	*31
Fish (salmon, shark, etc.)...........................	*126	*100	*80	*64	...	...
Marine mammals (whales, dolphins, etc.)	...	...	...	...	...	...
Other wildlife (butterflies, turtles, etc.)...............	293	100	*217	*74	*77	*26

* Estimate based on a sample size of 10–29.   ... Sample size too small to report data reliably.

Note: Detail does not add to total because of multiple responses.

Table 27. Participation in Wildlife-Watching Activities Around the Home in Alabama: 2006

(State population 16 years old and older. Numbers in thousands)

Around the home	Participants		Around the home	Participants	
	Number	Percent		Number	Percent
Total around-the-home participants...	**989**	**100**	11 to 50 days	*155	*23
Observe wildlife	676	68	51 to 200 days	229	34
Visit public parks[1]	*115	*12	201 days or more	*206	*31
Photograph wildlife	258	26			
Feed wildlife	924	93	**Participants Visiting Public Parks** [1]		
Maintain natural areas	*167	*17	Total, 1 day or more	*115	*100
Maintain plantings	*96	*10	1 to 5 days.....................	...	...
			6 to 10 days	...	...
Participants Observing Wildlife			11 days or more	...	...
Total, all wildlife.................	676	100			
Birds..........................	633	94	**Participants Photographing Wildlife**		
Land mammals..................	545	81	Total, 1 day or more	258	100
Large mammals	351	52	1 to 3 days.....................	*138	*53
Small mammals	466	69	4 to 10 days	...	...
Amphibians or reptiles	263	39	11 or more days	...	...
Insects or spiders	*179	*27			
Fish and other wildlife	*168	*25	**Participants Feeding Wildlife**		
			Total, all wildlife.................	924	100
Total, 1 day or more	676	100	Wild birds	911	99
1 to 10 days	...	...	Other wildlife	298	32

* Estimate based on a sample size of 10–29.   ... Sample size too small to report data reliably.

[1] Includes visits only to parks or publicly owned areas within 1 mile of home.

Note: Detail does not add to total because of multiple responses and nonresponse.

Table 28. Alabama Residents Participating in Wildlife Watching in the United States: 2006

(State population 16 years old and older. Numbers in thousands)

Participants	Number	Percent of participants	Percent of population
Total participants	**1,006**	**100**	**28**
Away from home	348	35	10
Around the home	989	98	28
Observe wildlife...	676	67	19
Photograph wildlife	258	26	7
Feed wild birds or other wildlife..............................	924	92	26
Maintain plantings or natural areas............................	*185	*18	*5
Visit public parks...	*115	*11	*3

* Estimate based on a sample size of 10–29.

Note: Detail does not add to total because of multiple responses. The column showing percent of participants is based on total participants. The column showing percent of population is based on the state population 16 years old and older, including those who did not participate in wildlife watching.

Table 29. Wild Bird Observers and Days of Observation in Alabama by State Residents and Nonresidents: 2006

(Population 16 years old and older. Numbers in thousands)

Observers and days of observation	Total, state residents and nonresidents		State residents		Nonresidents	
	Number	Percent	Number	Percent	Number	Percent
OBSERVERS						
Total bird observers........................	**828**	**100**	**687**	**100**	***141**	***100**
Around-the-home observers................	633	76	633	92	...	...
Away-from-home observers................	404	49	264	38	*141	*100
DAYS						
Total days observing birds	**85,644**	**100**	**85,099**	**100**	***545**	***100**
Around the home........................	82,537	96	82,537	97	...	...
Away from home........................	3,107	4	2,562	3	*545	*100

* Estimate based on a sample size of 10–29.   ... Sample size too small to report data reliably.

Note: Detail does not add to total because of multiple responses.

(State population 16 years old and older. Numbers in thousands)

Characteristic	Population		Participants									
			Total			Away from home			Around the home			
	Number	Percent	Number	Percent who partici-pated	Percent	Number	Percent who partici-pated	Percent	Number	Percent who partici-pated	Percent
Total persons....................	3,550	100	1,006	28	100	348	10	100	989	28	100
Population Density of Residence											
Urban	1,931	54	420	22	42	*148	*8	*43	420	22	42
Rural........................	1,620	46	586	36	58	*200	*12	*57	570	35	58
Population Size of Residence											
Metropolitan statistical area											
(MSA)......................	2,598	73	751	29	75	279	11	80	735	28	74
1,000,000 or more	981	28	356	36	35	*115	*12	*33	356	36	36
250,000 to 999,999	946	27	*239	*25	*24	*92	*10	*26	*222	*24	*22
Less than 250,000	671	19	*156	*23	*16	...	...	...	*156	*23	*16
Outside MSA	952	27	*255	*27	*25	...	...	...	*255	*27	*26
Sex											
Male........................	1,658	47	469	28	47	*153	*9	*44	453	27	46
Female	1,892	53	537	28	53	*195	*10	*56	537	28	54
Age											
16 to 17 years	137	4	...	...	...	...	...	...	...	...	...
18 to 24 years	307	9	...	...	...	...	...	...	...	...	...
25 to 34 years	513	14	*114	*22	*11	...	...	...	*114	*22	*12
35 to 44 years	592	17	*183	*31	*18	*82	*14	*24	*183	*31	*19
45 to 54 years	806	23	261	32	26	...	...	...	261	32	26
55 to 64 years	531	15	*166	*31	*16	...	...	...	*150	*28	*15
65 years and older	664	19	*227	*34	*23	...	...	...	*227	*34	*23
Ethnicity											
Hispanic	66	2	...	...	...	...	...	...	...	...	...
Non-Hispanic	3,485	98	997	29	99	348	10	100	981	28	99
Race											
White	2,649	75	888	34	88	315	12	90	872	33	88
Black........................	845	24	*101	*12	*10	...	...	...	*101	*12	*10
All others	*57	*2	...	...	...	...	...	...	...	...	...
Annual Household Income											
Under $10,000	259	7	...	...	...	...	...	...	...	...	...
$10,000 to $19,999	304	9	...	...	...	...	...	...	...	...	...
$20,000 to $29,999	454	13	*149	*33	*15	...	...	...	*149	*33	*15
$30,000 to $39,999	376	11	*115	*31	*11	...	...	...	*115	*31	*12
$40,000 to $49,999	350	10	...	...	...	...	...	...	...	...	...
$50,000 to $74,999	511	14	*166	*32	*17	...	...	...	*166	*32	*17
$75,000 to $99,999	251	7	*104	*41	*10	...	...	...	*104	*41	*10
$100,000 or more.............	292	8	*141	*48	*14	*88	*30	*25	*125	*43	*13
Not reported..................	753	21	*151	*20	*15	...	...	...	*151	*20	*15
Education											
11 years or less	775	22	*170	*22	*17	...	...	...	*170	*22	*17
12 years	1,238	35	322	26	32	...	...	...	322	26	33
1 to 3 years college	865	24	*216	*25	*21	*122	*14	*35	*216	*25	*22
4 years college or more..........	672	19	298	44	30	*130	*19	*37	282	42	28

* Estimate based on a sample size of 10–29.   ... Sample size too small to report data reliably.

Note: Detail does not add to total because of multiple responses and nonresponse. Percent who participated shows the percent of each row's population who participated in the activity named by the column (the percent of those living in urban areas who participated, etc.). Percent columns show the percent of each column's participants who are described by the row heading (the percent of those who participated who live in urban areas, etc.).

Table 31. Expenditures in Alabama by State Residents and Nonresidents Combined for Wildlife Watching: 2006

(Population 16 years old and older)

Expenditure item	Expenditures (thousands of dollars)	Average per participant (dollars)	Spenders		
			Number (thousands)	Percent of wildlife-watching participants[1]	Average per spender (dollars)
Total, all items......................................	450,004	377	983	85	458
TRIP EXPENDITURES					
Total trip-related.................................	151,665	309	393	83	386
Food and lodging	77,815	165	380	81	205
Food..	57,864	123	380	81	152
Lodging...................................	...	...	...	...	...
Transportation	47,239	87	341	72	139
Other trip costs[2]	*26,611	*56	*113	*24	*235
EQUIPMENT AND OTHER EXPENDITURES					
Total	298,339	251	866	75	344
Wildlife-watching equipment, total....................	137,632	117	844	73	163
Binoculars, spotting scopes	...	...	...	...	...
Film and developing...............................	*13,783	*12	*179	*15	*77
Cameras, special lenses, video cameras, and other photographic equipment	*18,910	*16	*80	*7	*237
Day packs, carrying cases, and special clothing	...	...	...	...	...
Bird food....................................	57,101	49	745	64	77
Food for other wildlife............................	*12,873	*11	*196	*17	*66
Nest boxes, bird houses, bird feeders, and bird baths.......	11,314	9	249	21	46
Other equipment (including field guides)	...	...	...	...	...
Auxiliary equipment[3]	...	...	...	...	...
Special equipment[4]	...	...	...	...	...
Magazines and books	*5,875	*5	*92	*8	*64
Membership dues and contributions.....................	...	...	...	...	...
Land leasing and ownership...........................	...	...	...	...	...
Plantings	*7,867	*7	*79	*7	*99

* Estimate based on a sample size of 10–29.   ... Sample size too small to report data reliably.

[1] Percent of wildlife-watching participants column for trip-related expenditures is based on away-from-home participants. For equipment and other expenditures, the percent of wildlife-watching participants column is based on total wildlife-watching participants.
[2] Includes equipment rental and fees for guides, pack trips, public land use and private land use, boat fuel, other boating costs, and heating and cooking fuel.
[3] Includes tents, tarps, frame packs and other backpacking equipment, other camping equipment, and other auxiliary equipment.
[4] Includes travel or tent trailers, off-the-road vehicles, pickups, campers or vans, motor homes, boats, and other special equipment.

Note: Detail does not add to total because of multiple responses and nonresponse.

Table 32. **Trip and Equipment Expenditures in Alabama for Wildlife Watching by Alabama Residents and Nonresidents: 2006**

(Population 16 years old and older)

Expenditure item	Amount (thousands of dollars)	Spenders (thousands)	Average per spender (dollars)	Average per participant (dollars)
STATE RESIDENTS AND NONRESIDENTS				
Total..	**410,216**	**970**	**423**	**346**
Food and lodging...................................	77,815	380	205	165
Transportation..	47,239	341	139	87
Other trip costs[1].....................................	*26,611	*113	*235	*56
Equipment[2]...	258,551	849	305	221
STATE RESIDENTS				
Total..	**349,915**	**846**	**414**	**342**
Food and lodging...................................	44,652	280	159	142
Transportation..	33,289	277	120	86
Other trip costs[1].....................................	...	...	...	...
Equipment[2]...	256,495	816	314	255
NONRESIDENTS				
Total..	***60,301**	***125**	***483**	***374**
Food and lodging...................................	*33,163	*100	*333	*213
Transportation..	...	...	...	...
Other trip costs[1].....................................	...	...	...	...
Equipment[2]...	...	...	...	...

* Estimate based on a sample size of 10–29.   ... Sample size too small to report data reliably.

[1] Includes equipment rental and fees for guides, pack trips, public land use, private land use, boat fuel, other boating costs, and heating and cooking fuel.
[2] Includes wildlife watching, auxiliary, and special equipment.

Note: Detail does not add to total because of multiple responses and nonresponse. See Table 33 for a detailed listing of expenditure items.

Table 33. Wildlife-Watching Expenditures Both Inside and Outside Alabama by Alabama Residents: 2006

(State population 16 years old and older)

Expenditure item	Expenditures (thousands of dollars)	Average per participant (dollars)	Spenders		
			Number (thousands)	Percent of wildlife-watching participants[1]	Average per spender (dollars)
Total, all items....................................	**493,849**	**491**	**853**	**85**	**579**
TRIP EXPENDITURES					
Total trip-related..................................	**198,132**	**569**	**327**	**94**	**607**
Food and lodging	111,944	321	297	85	377
Food..	59,017	169	292	84	202
Lodging.......................................	...	...	...	...	...
Transportation....................................	70,120	201	310	89	226
Other trip costs[2]	...	...	...	...	...
EQUIPMENT AND OTHER EXPENDITURES					
Total	**295,717**	**294**	**828**	**82**	**357**
Wildlife-watching equipment, total.....................	**135,839**	**135**	**811**	**81**	**167**
Binoculars, spotting scopes	...	...	...	...	...
Film and developing................................	*13,766	*14	*173	*17	*80
Cameras, special lenses, videocameras, and other photographic equipment	*18,910	*19	*80	*8	*237
Day packs, carrying cases, and special clothing	...	...	...	...	...
Bird food..	56,517	56	739	74	76
Food for other wildlife.............................	*12,837	*13	*189	*19	*68
Nest boxes, bird houses, bird feeders, and bird baths.......	*9,896	*10	*223	*22	*44
Other equipment..................................	...	...	...	...	...
Auxiliary equipment[3]	...	...	...	...	...
Special equipment[4].................................	...	...	...	...	...
Magazines and books...............................	*9,653	*10	*108	*11	*89
Membership dues and contributions.....................	...	...	...	...	...
Land leasing and ownership...........................	...	...	...	...	...
Plantings	*7,867	*8	*79	*8	*99

* Estimate based on a sample size of 10–29. ... Sample size too small to report data reliably.

[1] Percent of wildlife-watching participants column for trip-related expenditures is based on away-from-home participants. For equipment and other expenditures, the percent of wildlife-watching participants column is based on total wildlife-watching participants.
[2] Includes equipment rental and fees for guides, pack trips, public land use and private land use, boat fuel, other boating costs, and heating and cooking fuel.
[3] Includes tents, tarps, frame packs and other backpacking equipment, other camping equipment, and other auxiliary equipment.
[4] Includes travel or tent trailers, off-the-road vehicles, pickups, campers or vans, motor homes, boats, and other special equipment.

Note: Detail does not add to total because of multiple responses and nonresponse.

(State population 16 years old and older)

Expenditure item	Amount (thousands of dollars)	Spenders (thousands)	Average per spender (dollars)	Average per participant (dollars)
IN ALABAMA				
Expenditures for wildlife watching, total	**385,096**	**853**	**452**	**383**
Trip-related expenditures.............................	93,420	294	318	296
Wildlife-watching equipment...........................	135,576	811	167	135
Auxiliary equipment	...	...	...	...
Special equipment	...	...	...	...
Other..	*35,182	*166	*212	*35
OUT OF STATE				
Expenditures for wildlife watching, total	***108,753**	***120**	***909**	***996**
Trip-related expenditures.............................	*104,712	*98	*1,067	*996
Wildlife-watching equipment...........................	...	...	...	...
Auxiliary equipment	...	...	...	...
Special equipment	...	...	...	...
Other..	...	...	...	...

* Estimate based on a sample size of 10–29.   ... Sample size too small to report data reliably.

Note: See Table 33 for detailed listing of expenditure items.

Table 35. Participation of Alabama Resident Wildlife-Watching Participants in Fishing and Hunting: 2006

(State population 16 years old and older. Numbers in thousands)

Participants	Total wildlife watchers		Wildlife-watching activity			
			Away from home		Around the home	
	Number	Percent	Number	Percent	Number	Percent
Total participants.........................	**1,006**	**100**	**348**	**100**	**989**	**100**
Wildlife-watching participants who:						
Did not fish or hunt......................	711	71	230	66	726	73
Fished or hunted	295	29	119	34	264	27
Fished................................	273	27	110	31	245	25
Hunted	146	15	61	18	131	13

Note: Detail does not add to total because of multiple responses and nonresponse.

Table 36. Participation of Alabama Resident Sportspersons in Wildlife-Watching Activities: 2006

(State population 16 years old and older. Numbers in thousands)

Sportspersons	Sportspersons		Anglers		Hunters	
	Number	Percent	Number	Percent	Number	Percent
Total sportspersons............................	**707**	**100**	**628**	**100**	**312**	**100**
Sportspersons who:						
Did not engage in wildlife-watching activities	412	58	355	57	166	53
Engaged in wildlife-watching activities............	295	42	273	43	146	47
Away from home	119	17	110	17	61	20
Around the home	264	37	245	39	131	42

Note: Detail does not add to total because of multiple responses and nonresponse.

Table 37. **Participation in Wildlife-Associated Recreation by State Residents Both Inside and Outside Their Resident State: 2006**

(Population 16 years old and older. Numbers in thousands)

Participant's state of residence	Population	Total participants		Sportspersons		Wildlife-watching participants	
		Number	Percent of population	Number	Percent of population	Number	Percent of population
United States, total...........	229,245	87,465	38	33,916	15	71,132	31
Alabama.......................	3,550	1,417	40	707	20	1,006	28
Alaska........................	499	288	58	149	30	207	42
Arizona.......................	4,585	1,233	27	418	9	988	22
Arkansas......................	2,156	1,082	50	551	26	859	40
California	27,299	6,804	25	1,783	7	5,799	21
Colorado......................	3,605	1,735	48	593	16	1,459	40
Connecticut...................	2,735	1,223	45	297	11	1,102	40
Delaware......................	669	256	38	85	13	212	32
Florida	14,233	4,626	33	2,004	14	3,520	25
Georgia.......................	6,910	2,415	35	1,161	17	1,819	26
Hawaii	1,014	227	22	100	10	160	16
Idaho.........................	1,102	564	51	259	24	432	39
Illinois.......................	9,767	2,886	30	1,109	11	2,355	24
Indiana	4,799	2,279	47	822	17	1,825	38
Iowa	2,339	1,306	56	518	22	1,111	48
Kansas	2,110	979	46	425	20	787	37
Kentucky	3,260	1,667	51	670	21	1,341	41
Louisiana	3,433	1,106	32	678	20	712	21
Maine	1,074	717	67	266	25	600	56
Maryland	4,333	1,549	36	521	12	1,334	31
Massachusetts.................	5,032	1,931	38	472	9	1,725	34
Michigan......................	7,804	3,651	47	1,371	18	2,947	38
Minnesota.....................	4,021	2,480	62	1,280	32	1,946	48
Mississippi	2,214	896	40	537	24	618	28
Missouri	4,521	2,496	55	1,096	24	2,059	46
Montana	753	510	68	232	31	412	55
Nebraska......................	1,359	552	41	234	17	438	32
Nevada	1,895	530	28	182	10	420	22
New Hampshire	1,044	527	51	141	14	471	45
New Jersey....................	6,734	1,826	27	562	8	1,537	23
New Mexico...................	1,500	601	40	224	15	490	33
New York.....................	14,990	4,103	27	1,236	8	3,548	24
North Carolina	6,719	2,816	42	1,038	15	2,267	34
North Dakota	507	232	46	145	29	134	26
Ohio	8,889	4,022	45	1,488	17	3,379	38
Oklahoma.....................	2,743	1,372	50	602	22	1,082	39
Oregon	2,889	1,531	53	550	19	1,266	44
Pennsylvania..................	9,793	4,165	43	1,415	14	3,638	37
Rhode Island	842	355	42	86	10	312	37
South Carolina	3,315	1,283	39	595	18	943	28
South Dakota	601	327	54	136	23	266	44
Tennessee	4,699	2,287	49	775	16	1,966	42
Texas.........................	17,076	5,481	32	2,668	16	4,111	24
Utah	1,808	764	42	351	19	574	32
Vermont	506	311	62	91	18	279	55
Virginia.......................	5,893	2,500	42	857	15	2,126	36
Washington....................	4,980	2,315	46	764	15	2,007	40
West Virginia	1,458	735	50	364	25	585	40
Wisconsin.....................	4,350	2,217	51	1,185	27	1,710	39
Wyoming	405	229	57	113	28	194	48

Note: Detail does not add to total because of multiple responses. U.S. totals include responses from participants residing in the District of Columbia, as described in Appendix D.

Table 30. Anglers and Hunters by Sportsperson's State of Residence: 2006

(Population 16 years old and older. Numbers in thousands)

Sportsperson's state of residence	Population	Fished or hunted		Fished only		Hunted only		Fished and hunted	
		Number	Percent of population	Number	Percent of population	Number	Percent of population	Number	Percent of population
United States, total.....	**229,245**	**33,916**	**15**	**21,406**	**9**	**3,964**	**2**	**8,546**	**4**
Alabama	3,550	707	20	395	11	79	2	233	7
Alaska.................	499	149	30	94	19	*11	*2	44	9
Arizona................	4,585	418	9	290	6	48	1	81	2
Arkansas..............	2,156	551	26	244	11	88	4	220	10
California	27,299	1,783	7	1,465	5	*94	*(Z)	223	1
Colorado..............	3,605	593	16	460	13	*39	*1	94	3
Connecticut............	2,735	297	11	257	9	...	...	34	1
Delaware..............	669	85	13	64	10	*9	*1	12	2
Florida	14,233	2,004	14	1,678	12	*54	*(Z)	271	2
Georgia...............	6,910	1,161	17	805	12	*101	*1	255	4
Hawaii	1,014	100	10	81	8	...	...	*14	*1
Idaho.................	1,102	259	24	136	12	*36	*3	88	8
Illinois................	9,767	1,109	11	837	9	*74	*1	198	2
Indiana	4,799	822	17	569	12	83	2	171	4
Iowa	2,339	518	22	308	13	70	3	141	6
Kansas	2,110	425	20	233	11	56	3	136	6
Kentucky	3,260	670	21	410	13	*49	*1	212	7
Louisiana	3,433	678	20	403	12	*81	*2	195	6
Maine	1,074	266	25	120	11	40	4	106	10
Maryland	4,333	521	12	370	9	46	1	105	2
Massachusetts...........	5,032	472	9	406	8	*20	*(Z)	46	1
Michigan..............	7,804	1,371	18	650	8	272	3	449	6
Minnesota.............	4,021	1,280	32	745	19	*138	*3	398	10
Mississippi	2,214	537	24	293	13	*58	*3	186	8
Missouri	4,521	1,096	24	536	12	165	4	394	9
Montana	753	232	31	86	11	53	7	92	12
Nebraska..............	1,359	234	17	129	10	42	3	63	5
Nevada	1,895	182	10	122	6	26	1	34	2
New Hampshire	1,044	141	14	89	9	*17	*2	35	3
New Jersey.............	6,734	562	8	478	7	*32	*(Z)	53	1
New Mexico............	1,500	224	15	152	10	34	2	38	3
New York.............	14,990	1,236	8	734	5	207	1	295	2
North Carolina	6,719	1,038	15	734	11	*74	*1	230	3
North Dakota	507	145	29	59	12	40	8	47	9
Ohio	8,889	1,488	17	1,011	11	195	2	282	3
Oklahoma..............	2,743	602	22	370	13	*55	*2	177	6
Oregon	2,889	550	19	331	11	67	2	152	5
Pennsylvania............	9,793	1,415	14	482	5	425	4	508	5
Rhode Island	842	86	10	73	9	...	...	*10	*1
South Carolina	3,315	595	18	429	13	*48	*1	119	4
South Dakota	601	136	23	46	8	41	7	50	8
Tennessee	4,699	775	16	491	10	*67	*1	217	5
Texas.................	17,076	2,668	16	1,672	10	324	2	672	4
Utah	1,808	351	19	197	11	38	2	116	6
Vermont	506	91	18	34	7	20	4	37	7
Virginia...............	5,893	857	15	497	8	127	2	233	4
Washington............	4,980	764	15	577	12	74	1	113	2
West Virginia	1,458	364	25	165	11	58	4	141	10
Wisconsin..............	4,350	1,185	27	534	12	160	4	492	11
Wyoming	405	113	28	61	15	*15	*4	37	9

* Estimate based on a sample size of 10–29.   ... Sample size too small to report data reliably.   (Z) Less than 0.5 percent.

Notes: U.S. totals include responses from participants residing in the District of Columbia, as described in Appendix D.

Table includes state residents' participation both inside and outside their resident state.

Table 39. Participation in Wildlife-Associated Recreation in Each State by Both Residents and Nonresidents of the State: 2006

(Population 16 years old and older. Numbers in thousands)

State where activity took place	Total participants		Sportspersons		Wildlife-watching participants	
	Number	Percent	Number	Percent	Number	Percent
United States, total..........	**87,465**	**100**	**33,916**	**39**	**71,132**	**81**
Alabama......................	1,719	100	962	56	1,161	68
Alaska........................	691	100	315	46	496	72
Arizona......................	1,546	100	493	32	1,277	83
Arkansas.....................	1,419	100	790	56	1,011	71
California	7,385	100	1,814	25	6,270	85
Colorado.....................	2,234	100	813	36	1,819	81
Connecticut...................	1,332	100	309	23	1,170	88
Delaware......................	395	100	189	48	285	72
Florida	5,886	100	2,815	48	4,240	72
Georgia......................	2,773	100	1,308	47	1,987	72
Hawaii	366	100	162	44	262	72
Idaho........................	1,005	100	440	44	754	75
Illinois.......................	3,126	100	1,004	32	2,566	82
Indiana	2,610	100	886	34	2,042	78
Iowa	1,455	100	552	38	1,205	83
Kansas	1,107	100	544	49	816	74
Kentucky	1,906	100	820	43	1,475	77
Louisiana	1,221	100	769	63	738	60
Maine	1,007	100	411	41	801	80
Maryland	1,867	100	707	38	1,491	80
Massachusetts..................	2,205	100	532	24	1,919	87
Michigan......................	4,217	100	1,685	40	3,227	77
Minnesota.....................	2,970	100	1,571	53	2,093	70
Mississippi	1,138	100	656	58	731	64
Missouri	2,876	100	1,300	45	2,248	78
Montana	950	100	378	40	755	79
Nebraska......................	650	100	259	40	490	75
Nevada	788	100	177	22	686	87
New Hampshire	839	100	258	31	710	85
New Jersey....................	2,100	100	696	33	1,713	82
New Mexico...................	947	100	316	33	787	83
New York	4,595	100	1,428	31	3,852	84
North Carolina	3,412	100	1,361	40	2,641	77
North Dakota	279	100	190	68	148	53
Ohio	4,247	100	1,488	35	3,489	82
Oklahoma.....................	1,472	100	684	46	1,110	75
Oregon	1,837	100	661	36	1,484	81
Pennsylvania...................	4,663	100	1,520	33	3,947	85
Rhode Island	527	100	163	31	436	83
South Carolina	1,653	100	893	54	1,115	67
South Dakota	572	100	251	44	432	75
Tennessee	2,824	100	969	34	2,362	84
Texas........................	6,029	100	2,940	49	4,225	70
Utah	1,132	100	437	39	877	77
Vermont	545	100	150	27	468	86
Virginia......................	2,866	100	1,045	36	2,312	81
Washington....................	2,739	100	818	30	2,331	85
West Virginia	994	100	488	49	743	75
Wisconsin.....................	2,913	100	1,582	54	2,039	70
Wyoming	762	100	264	35	643	84

Note: Detail does not add to total because of multiple responses. U.S. totals include responses from participants residing in the District of Columbia, as described in Appendix D.

Table 40. Anglers and Hunters by State Where Fishing or Hunting Took Place: 2006

(Population 16 years old and older. Numbers in thousands)

State where fishing or hunting took place	Anglers						Hunters					
	Total anglers, residents and nonresidents		Residents		Nonresidents		Total hunters, residents and nonresidents		Residents		Nonresidents	
	Number	Percent	Number	Percent	Number	Percent	Number	Percent	Number	Percent	Number	Percent
United States, total.....	29,952	100	27,641	92	6,494	22	12,510	100	11,971	96	1,826	15
Alabama	806	100	600	74	206	26	391	100	310	79	81	21
Alaska.................	293	100	137	47	156	53	71	100	53	75	...	...
Arizona...............	422	100	330	78	92	22	159	100	126	79	*33	*21
Arkansas..............	655	100	430	66	225	34	354	100	301	85	*53	*15
California	1,730	100	1,578	91	152	9	281	100	274	97	...	...
Colorado..............	660	100	490	74	171	26	259	100	126	49	134	51
Connecticut............	302	100	251	83	51	17	38	100	36	96	...	...
Delaware..............	159	100	66	41	*94	*59	42	100	19	46	...	...
Florida	2,767	100	1,881	68	885	32	236	100	214	91	*22	*9
Georgia...............	1,107	100	971	88	136	12	481	100	344	72	136	28
Hawaii	157	100	92	58	*65	*42	18	100	18	98	...	...
Idaho.................	350	100	206	59	144	41	187	100	122	65	65	35
Illinois................	873	100	795	91	78	9	316	100	258	82	*58	*18
Indiana	768	100	663	86	106	14	272	100	237	87	*35	*13
Iowa	438	100	397	91	*40	*9	251	100	208	83	*44	*17
Kansas	404	100	319	79	85	21	271	100	183	68	88	32
Kentucky	721	100	580	80	141	20	291	100	241	83	*50	*17
Louisiana	702	100	590	84	112	16	270	100	241	89	...	...
Maine	351	100	220	63	131	37	175	100	146	83	*29	*17
Maryland	645	100	403	62	242	38	161	100	133	83	*28	*17
Massachusetts..........	497	100	398	80	99	20	73	100	57	79	*16	*21
Michigan..............	1,394	100	1,077	77	318	23	753	100	721	96	*32	*4
Minnesota.............	1,427	100	1,108	78	319	22	535	100	509	95	*26	*5
Mississippi	546	100	465	85	80	15	304	100	238	78	*66	*22
Missouri	1,076	100	871	81	206	19	608	100	540	89	69	11
Montana	291	100	172	59	119	41	197	100	145	74	*52	*26
Nebraska..............	198	100	169	85	*29	*15	118	100	102	86	...	...
Nevada	142	100	114	81	*27	*19	63	100	54	85	...	...
New Hampshire	230	100	108	47	122	53	61	100	51	85	*9	*15
New Jersey.............	654	100	458	70	197	30	89	100	72	81	...	...
New Mexico............	248	100	164	66	*84	*34	99	100	66	67	*32	*33
New York..............	1,153	100	932	81	221	19	566	100	491	87	75	13
North Carolina	1,263	100	868	69	395	31	304	100	277	91	*27	*9
North Dakota	106	100	88	84	...	...	128	100	86	67	*42	*33
Ohio	1,256	100	1,145	91	112	9	500	100	467	93	...	...
Oklahoma.............	611	100	525	86	86	14	251	100	224	89	*27	*11
Oregon	576	100	455	79	122	21	237	100	218	92	...	...
Pennsylvania...........	994	100	830	83	164	17	1,044	100	933	89	111	11
Rhode Island	158	100	76	48	82	52	14	100	12	84	...	...
South Carolina	810	100	527	65	283	35	208	100	159	77	*49	*23
South Dakota	135	100	89	66	45	34	171	100	89	52	81	48
Tennessee	871	100	658	75	214	25	329	100	265	81	*64	*19
Texas.................	2,527	100	2,308	91	218	9	1,101	100	979	89	123	11
Utah	375	100	288	77	87	23	166	100	144	86	*23	*14
Vermont	114	100	64	56	50	44	73	100	56	76	*17	*24
Virginia...............	858	100	640	75	218	25	413	100	353	86	*60	*14
Washington............	736	100	641	87	95	13	182	100	179	98	...	...
West Virginia	376	100	291	77	86	23	269	100	194	72	*75	*28
Wisconsin	1,394	100	1,014	73	381	27	697	100	649	93	*48	*7
Wyoming	203	100	96	47	107	53	102	100	50	49	52	51

* Estimate based on a sample size of 10–29.   ... Sample size too small to report data reliably.

Note: Detail does not add to total because of multiple responses. U.S. totals include responses from participants residing in the District of Columbia, as described in Appendix D.

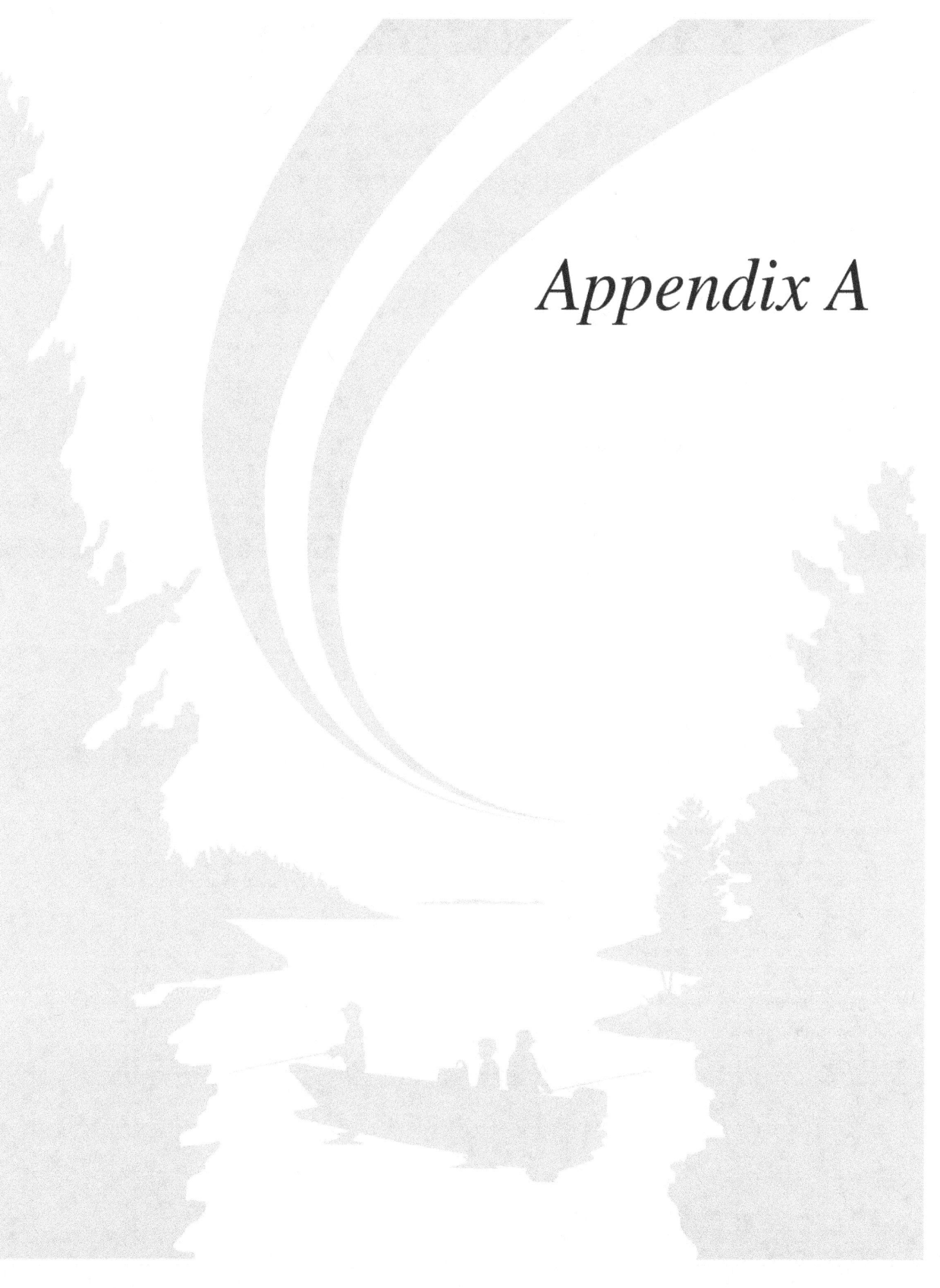

Appendix A

Appendix A.
Definitions

Annual household income—Total 2006 income of household members before taxes and other deductions.

Around-the-home wildlife watching—Activity within 1 mile of home with one of six primary purposes: (1) taking special interest in or trying to identify birds or other wildlife; (2) photographing wildlife; (3) feeding birds or other wildlife; (4) maintaining natural areas of at least 1/4 acre for the benefit of wildlife; (5) maintaining plantings (such as shrubs and agricultural crops) for the benefit of wildlife; and (6) visiting public land to observe, photograph, or feed wildlife.

Auxiliary equipment—Equipment owned primarily for wildlife-associated recreation. For the sportspersons section, these include sleeping bags, packs, duffel bags, tents, binoculars and field glasses, special fishing and hunting clothing, foul weather gear, boots and waders, maintenance and repair of equipment, and processing and taxidermy costs. For the wildlife-watching section, these include tents, tarps, frame packs, backpacking and other camping equipment, and blinds.

Away-from-home wildlife watching—Trips or outings at least 1 mile from home for the primary purpose of observing, photographing, or feeding wildlife. Trips to zoos, circuses, aquariums, and museums are not included.

Big game—Bear, deer, elk, moose, wild turkey, and similar large animals that are hunted.

Census Divisions
East North Central
Illinois
Indiana
Michigan
Ohio
Wisconsin

East South Central
Alabama
Kentucky
Mississippi
Tennessee

Middle Atlantic
New Jersey
New York
Pennsylvania

Mountain
Arizona
Colorado
Idaho
Montana
Nevada
New Mexico
Utah
Wyoming

New England
Connecticut
Maine
Massachusetts
New Hampshire
Rhode Island
Vermont

Pacific
Alaska
California
Hawaii
Oregon
Washington

South Atlantic
Delaware
District of Columbia
Florida
Georgia
Maryland
North Carolina
South Carolina
Virginia
West Virginia

West North Central
Kansas
Iowa
Minnesota
Missouri
Nebraska
North Dakota
South Dakota

West South Central
Arkansas
Louisiana
Oklahoma
Texas

Day—Any part of a day spent participating in a given activity. For example, if someone hunted two hours one day and three hours another day, it would be reported as two days of hunting. If someone hunted two hours in the morning and three hours in the afternoon of the same day, it would be considered one day of hunting.

Education—The highest completed grade of school or year of college.

Expenditures—Money spent in 2006 for wildlife-related recreation trips in the United States, wildlife-related recreational equipment purchased in the United States, and other items. The "other items" were books and magazines, membership dues and contributions, land leasing or owning, hunting and fishing licenses, and plantings, all for the purpose of wildlife-related recreation. Expenditures included both money spent by participants for themselves and the value of gifts they received.

Fishing—The sport of catching or attempting to catch fish with a hook and line, bow and arrow, or spear; it also includes catching or gathering shellfish (clams, crabs, etc.); and the noncommercial seining or netting of fish, unless the fish are for use as bait. For example, seining for smelt is fishing, but seining for bait minnows is not included as fishing.

Fishing equipment—Items owned primarily for fishing:

Rods, reels, poles, and rodmaking components

Lines and leaders

Artificial lures, flies, baits, and dressing for flies or lines

Hooks, sinkers, swivels, and other items attached to a line, except lures and baits

Tackle boxes

Creels, stringers, fish bags, landing nets, and gaff hooks

Minnow traps, seines, and bait containers

Depth finders, fish finders, and other electronic fishing devices

Ice fishing equipment

Other fishing equipment

Freshwater—Reservoirs, lakes, ponds, and the nontidal portions of rivers and streams.

Great Lakes fishing—Fishing in Lakes Superior, Michigan, Huron, St. Clair, Erie, and Ontario, their connecting waters such as the St. Mary's River system, Detroit River, St. Clair River, and the Niagara River, and the St. Lawrence River south of the bridge at Cornwall, New York. Great Lakes fishing includes fishing in tributaries of the Great Lakes for smelt, steelhead, and salmon.

Home—The starting point of a wildlife-related recreational trip. It may be a permanent residence or a temporary or seasonal residence such as a cabin.

Hunting—The sport of shooting or attempting to shoot wildlife with firearms or archery equipment.

Hunting equipment—Items owned primarily for hunting:

Rifles, shotguns, muzzleloaders, and handguns

Archery equipment

Telescopic sights

Decoys and game calls

Ammunition

Hand loading equipment

Hunting dogs and associated costs

Other hunting equipment

Land leasing and owning—Leasing or owning land either singly or in cooperation with others for the primary purpose of fishing, hunting, or wildlife watching on it.

Maintain natural areas—To set aside 1/4 acre or more of natural environment, such as wood lots or open fields, for the primary purpose of benefiting wildlife. This is categorized as a wildlife-watching activity, not fishing or hunting.

Maintain plantings—To introduce or encourage the growth of food and cover plants for the primary purpose of benefiting wildlife. Examples of plantings are butterfly bushes and various sumacs. This is categorized as a wildlife-watching activity, not fishing or hunting.

Metropolitan statistical area (MSA)—Except in the New England States, an MSA is a county or group of contiguous counties containing at least one city of 50,000 or more inhabitants or twin cities (i.e., cities with contiguous boundaries and constituting, for general social and economic purposes, a single community) with a combined population of at least 50,000. Also included in an MSA are contiguous counties that are socially and economically integrated with the central city. In the New England States, an MSA consists of towns and cities instead of counties. Each MSA must include at least one central city. See U.S. Census Bureau publication *State and Metropolitan Area Data Book; 2006* for more detailed information on MSAs. It can be found at <http://www.census.gov /prod/2006pubs/smadb/smadb-06.pdf>.

Migratory birds—Birds that regularly migrate from one region or climate to another such as ducks, geese, and doves and other birds that may be hunted.

Multiple responses—The term used to reflect the fact that individuals or their characteristics fall into more than one reporting category. An example of a big game hunter who hunted for deer and elk demonstrates the effect of multiple responses. In this case, adding the number of deer hunters (one) and elk hunters (one) would overstate the number of big game hunters (one)

because deer and elk hunters are not mutually exclusive categories. In contrast, total participants is the sum of male and female participants, because "male" and "female" are mutually exclusive categories.

Nonresidents—Individuals who do not live in the State being reported. For example, a person living in Texas who watches whales in California is a nonresidential wildlife-watcher in California.

Nonresponse—A term used to reflect the fact that some Survey respondents provide incomplete sets of information. For example, a Survey respondent may have been unable to identify the primary type of hunting for which a gun was bought. Total hunting expenditure estimates will include the gun purchase, but it will not appear as spending for big game or any other type of hunting. Nonresponses result in reported totals that are greater than the sum of their parts.

Observe—To take special interest in or try to identify birds, fish, or other wildlife.

Other animals—Coyotes, crows, foxes, groundhogs, prairie dogs, raccoons, and similar animals that can be legally hunted and are not classified as big game, small game, or migratory birds. They may be classified as unprotected or predatory animals by the State in which they are hunted. Feral pigs are classified as "other animals" in all States except Hawaii, where they are considered big game.

Participants—Individuals who engage in fishing, hunting, or a wildlife-watching activity. Unless otherwise stated, a person has to have hunted, fished, or wildlife watched in 2006 to be considered a participant.

Plantings—See "Maintain plantings."

Primary purpose—The principal motivation for an activity, trip, or expenditure.

Private land—Land that is owned by a private individual, group of individuals, or nongovernmental organization.

Public land—Land that is owned by local governments (such as county parks and municipal watersheds), State governments (such as State parks and wildlife management areas), or federal governments (such as National Forests and Wildlife Refuges).

Public parks or areas—See "Public land."

Residents—Individuals who lived in the State being reported. For example, a person who lives in California and watches whales in California is a residential wildlife watcher in California.

Rural—All territory, population, and housing units located outside of urbanized areas and urban clusters, as determined by the Census Bureau.

Saltwater—Oceans, tidal bays and sounds, and the tidal portions of rivers and streams.

Screening interviews—The first Survey contact with a sample household. Screening interviews are conducted with a household representative to identify respondents who are eligible for in-depth interviews. Screening interviews gather data such as age and sex about individuals in the households. Further information on screening interviews is available on page vii in the "Survey Background and Method" section of this report.

Small game—Grouse, pheasants, quail, rabbits, squirrels, and similar small animals for which States have small game seasons and bag limits.

Special equipment—Big-ticket equipment items that are owned primarily for wildlife-related recreation:

Bass boats

Other types of motorboats

Canoes and other types of non-motorboats

Boat motors, boat trailer/hitches, and other boat accessories

Pickups, campers, vans, travel or tent trailers, motor homes, house trailers, recreational vehicles (RVs)

Cabins

Off-the-road vehicles such as trail bikes, all terrain vehicles (ATVs), dune buggies, four-wheelers, 4x4 vehicles, and snowmobiles

Other special equipment

Spenders—People who spent money on fishing, hunting, or wildlife-watching activities or equipment.

Sportspersons—Individuals who engage in fishing, hunting, or both.

Trip—An outing involving fishing, hunting, or wildlife watching. A trip may begin from an individual's principal residence or from another place, such as a vacation home or the home of a relative. A trip may last an hour, a day, or many days.

Type of fishing—There are three types of fishing: (1) freshwater except Great Lakes, (2) Great Lakes, and (3) saltwater.

Type of hunting—There are four types of hunting: (1) big game, (2) small game, (3) migratory bird, and (4) other animal.

Unspecified expenditure—An item that was purchased for use in both fishing and hunting, rather than primarily one or the other. Auxiliary equipment, special equipment, magazines and books, and membership dues and contributions are the items for which a purchase could be categorized as "unspecified."

Urban—All territory, population, and housing units located within boundaries that encompass densely settled territory, consisting of core census block groups or blocks that have a population density of at least 1,000 people per square mile and surrounding census blocks that have an overall density of at least 500 people per square mile. Under certain conditions, less densely settled territory may be included, as determined by the Census Bureau.

Wildlife—Animals, such as birds, fish, insects, mammals, amphibians, and reptiles that are living in natural or wild environments. Wildlife does not include animals living in aquariums, zoos, and other artificial surroundings or domestic animals such as farm animals or pets.

Wildlife-associated recreation—Recreational fishing, hunting, and wildlife watching.

Wildlife watching—There are six types of wildlife watching: (1) closely observing, (2) photographing, (3) feeding, (4) visiting public parks or areas, (5) maintaining plantings, and (6) maintaining natural areas. These activities must be the primary purpose of the trip or the around-the-home undertaking.

Wildlife observed, photographed, or fed—Examples of species that wildlife watchers observe, photograph, and/or feed are (1) Wild birds—songbirds such as cardinals, robins, warblers, jays, buntings, and sparrows; birds of prey such as hawks, owls, eagles, and falcons; waterfowl such as ducks, geese, and swans; other water birds such as shorebirds, herons, pelicans, and cranes; and other birds such as pheasants, turkeys, road runners, and woodpeckers; (2) Land mammals—large land mammals such as bears, bison, deer, moose, and elk; and small land mammals such as squirrels, foxes, prairie dogs, and rabbits; (3) Fish such as salmon, sharks, and groupers; (4) Marine mammals such as whales, dolphins, and manatees; and (5) Other wildlife such as butterflies, turtles, spiders, and snakes.

Wildlife-watching equipment—Items owned primarily for observing, photographing, or feeding wildlife:

Binoculars and spotting scopes

Cameras, video cameras, special lenses, and other photographic equipment

Film and developing

Commercially prepared and packaged wild bird food

Other bulk food used to feed wild birds

Food for other wildlife

Nest boxes, bird houses, feeders, and baths

Day packs, carrying cases, and special clothing

Other items such as field guides and maps

Appendix B

Appendix B.
2005 Participation of 6- to 15-Year-Olds: Data From Screening Interviews

The *2006 National Survey of Fishing, Hunting, and Wildlife-Associated Recreation* was carried out in two phases. The first (or screening) phase began in April 2006. The main purpose of this phase was to collect information about all persons 16 years old and older in order to develop a sample of potential sportspersons and wildlife watchers for the second (or detailed) phase. Also, information was collected on the number of persons 6 to 15 years old who participated in wildlife-related recreation activities in 2005.

It is important to emphasize that the information reported from the 2006 screen relates to activity only up to and including 2005. Also, these data are reported in most cases by one household respondent speaking for all household members rather than the actual participant. In addition, these data are based on long-term recall (at least a 12-month recall), which has been found in Survey research (Investigation of Possible Recall/Reference Period Bias in National Surveys of Fishing, Hunting, and Wildlife-Associated Recreation, December 1989, Westat, Inc.) to add bias to the resulting estimates. In many cases, longer recall periods result in overestimating participation and expenditures for wildlife-related recreation.

Tables B-1 through B-4 report data on 6-to-15-year-old participants in 2005. Detailed expenditure and recreational activity data were not gathered for the 6-to-15-year-old participants.

Because of differences in methodologies of the screening and the detailed phases of the 2006 Survey, resulting estimates are not comparable. Only participants 16 years old and older were eligible for the detailed phase. The detailed phase was a series of three interviews conducted at four-month intervals. The screening interviews were one year or more recall. The shorter recall period of the detailed phase had better data accuracy.

Table B-1. **Alabama Residents 6 to 15 Years Old Participating in Fishing and Hunting Both Inside and Outside Alabama: 2005**

(State population 6 to 15 years old. Numbers in thousands)

Sportspersons	Sportspersons 6 to 15 years old		
	Number	Percent of sportspersons	Percent of population
Total sportspersons	**230**	**100**	**38**
Total anglers	**220**	**96**	**37**
Fished only...	157	68	26
Fished and hunted	*64	*28	*11
Total hunters..	**73**	**32**	**12**
Hunted only	...	...	...
Hunted and fished	*64	*28	*11

* Estimate based on a sample size of 10–29.   ... Sample size too small to report data reliably.

Note: Detail does not add to total because of multiple responses. Column showing percent of sportspersons is based on the "Total sportspersons" row. Column showing percent of population is based on the state population 6 to 15 years old, including those who did not fish or hunt. Data reported on this table are from screening interviews in which one adult household member responded for household members 6 to 15 years old. The screening interview required the respondent to recall 12 months worth of activity. Includes state residents who fished or hunted only in other countries.

(State population 6 to 15 years old. Numbers in thousands)

Characteristic	Population		Sportspersons (fished or hunted)			Anglers			Hunters		
	Number	Percent	Number	Percent who partici-pated	Percent	Number	Percent who partici-pated	Percent	Number	Percent who partici-pated	Percent
Total persons	600	100	230	38	100	220	37	100	73	12	100
Population Density of Residence											
Urban.	355	59	114	32	50	111	31	51	*31	*9	*43
Rural	245	41	116	47	50	109	44	49	*42	*17	*57
Population Size of Residence											
Metropolitan statistical areas (MSA)	437	73	161	37	70	153	35	69	*48	*11	*66
1,000,000 or more	140	23	70	50	30	70	50	32	...	...	...
250,000 to 999,999.	193	32	*42	*22	*18	*41	*21	*18	...	...	...
Less than 250,000.	103	17	*49	*48	*21	*43	*41	*19	...	...	...
Outside MSA	163	27	*69	*42	*30	*67	*41	*31	*25	*15	*34
Sex											
Male	314	52	146	46	63	136	43	62	*50	*16	*68
Female.	286	48	84	29	37	84	29	38	*24	*8	*32
Age											
6 to 8 years.	192	32	*54	*28	*23	*54	*28	*24	...	...	...
9 to 11 years.	142	24	61	43	27	*57	*40	*26	...	...	...
12 to 15 years.	266	44	115	43	50	109	41	50	*43	*16	*59
Ethnicity											
Hispanic	...	...	...	...	...	...	...	...	...	...	...
Non-Hispanic	589	98	230	39	100	220	37	100	73	12	100
Race											
White.	383	64	199	52	86	189	49	86	71	19	97
Black.	197	33	...	...	...	...	...	...	...	...	...
All others	...	...	...	...	...	...	...	...	...	...	...
Annual Household Income											
Less than $10,000.	100	17	...	...	...	...	...	...	...	...	...
$10,000 to $19,999.	72	12	...	...	...	...	...	...	...	...	...
$20,000 to $29,999.	80	13	*41	*51	*18	*35	*44	*16	...	...	...
$30,000 to $39,999.	*53	*9	...	...	...	...	...	...	...	...	...
$40,000 to $49,999.	*40	*7	*23	*57	*10	*23	*57	*10	...	...	...
$50,000 to $74,999.	95	16	*47	*49	*20	*45	*48	*21	*22	*23	*30
$75,000 or more	104	17	*36	*35	*16	*36	*35	*16	...	...	...
Not reported	57	9	*30	*53	*13	*30	*53	*14	...	...	...

* Estimate based on a sample size of 10–29.   ... Sample size too small to report data reliably.

Note: Percent who participated shows the percent of each row's population who participated in the activity named by the column (the percent of those living in urban areas who fished, etc.). Remaining percent columns show the percent of each column's participants who are described by the row heading (the percent of anglers who lived in urban areas, etc.). Data reported on this table are from screening interviews in which one adult household member responded for 6 to 15 years old. The screening interview required the respondent to recall 12 months worth of activity. Includes state residents who fished or hunted only in other countries.

Table B-3. **Alabama Residents 6 to 15 Years Old Participating in Wildlife Watching Both Inside and Outside Alabama: 2005**

(State population 6 to 15 years old. Numbers in thousands)

Participants	Number	Percent of participants	Percent of population
Total participants	177	100	29
Away from home	*49	*27	*8
Around the home	165	93	27
Observe wildlife	133	75	22
Photograph wildlife	*24	*14	*4
Feed wild birds or other wildlife	92	52	15
Maintain plantings or natural areas	*32	*18	*5

* Estimate based on a sample size of 10–29.

Note: Detail does not add to total because of multiple responses. The column showing percent of participants is based on total participants. The column showing percent of population is based on the state population 6 to 15 years old, including those who did not participate in wildlife watching. Data reported on this table are from screening interviews in which one adult household member responded for household members 6 to 15 years old. The screening interview required the respondent to recall 12 months worth of activity. Includes state residents who wildlife watched only in other countries.

(State population 6 to 15 years old. Numbers in thousands)

Characteristic	Population		Total wildlife watchers			Away from home			Around the home		
	Number	Percent	Number	Percent who partici-pated	Percent	Number	Percent who partici-pated	Percent	Number	Percent who partici-pated	Percent
Total persons	600	100	177	29	100	*49	*8	*100	165	27	100
Population Density of Residence											
Urban.................	355	59	91	26	52	*30	*9	*62	82	23	50
Rural	245	41	86	35	48	...	...	...	83	34	50
Population Size of Residence											
Metropolitan statistical areas (MSA).................	437	73	132	30	75	*35	*8	*73	121	28	74
1,000,000 or more	140	23	*52	*38	*30	...	...	...	*51	*36	*31
250,000 to 999,999......	193	32	*46	*24	*26	...	...	...	*37	*19	*22
Less than 250,000.......	103	17	*33	*32	*19	...	...	...	*33	*32	*20
Outside MSA	163	27	*45	*28	*25	...	...	...	*44	*27	*26
Sex											
Male	314	52	93	30	53	*26	*8	*53	88	28	53
Female.................	286	48	84	29	47	*23	*8	*47	77	27	47
Age											
6 to 8 years..............	192	32	*55	*29	*31	...	...	...	*49	*26	*30
9 to 11 years.............	142	24	*46	*32	*26	...	...	...	*44	*31	*26
12 to 15 years............	266	44	76	28	43	*24	*9	*50	72	27	44
Ethnicity											
Hispanic	...	...	...	...	...	...	...	...	...	...	...
Non-Hispanic	589	98	177	30	100	*49	*8	*100	165	28	100
Race											
White...................	383	64	126	33	71	*42	*11	*86	113	30	69
Black...................	197	33	*38	*19	*21	...	...	...	*38	*19	*23
All others	...	...	...	...	...	...	...	...	...	...	...
Annual Household Income											
Less than $10,000.	100	17	...	...	...	...	...	...	...	...	...
$10,000 to $19,999........	72	12	...	...	...	...	...	...	...	...	...
$20,000 to $29,999........	80	13	...	...	...	...	...	...	...	...	...
$30,000 to $39,999........	*53	*9	...	...	...	...	...	...	...	...	...
$40,000 to $49,999........	*40	*7	...	...	...	...	...	...	...	...	...
$50,000 to $74,999........	95	16	*39	*41	*22	...	...	...	*37	*39	*23
$75,000 or more	104	17	*48	*46	*27	...	...	...	*43	*41	*26
Not reported	57	9	...	...	...	...	...	...	...	...	...

* Estimate based on a sample size of 10–29.   ... Sample size too small to report data reliably.

Note: Percent who participated shows the percent of each row's population who participated in the activity named by the column (the percent of those living in urban areas who wildlife watched, etc.). Remaining percent columns show the percent of each column's participants who are described by the row heading (the percent of wildlife watchers who lived in urban areas, etc.). Data reported on this table are from screening interviews in which one adult household member responded for 6 to 15 years old. The screening interview required the respondent to recall 12 months worth of activity. Includes state residents who wildlife watched only in other countries.

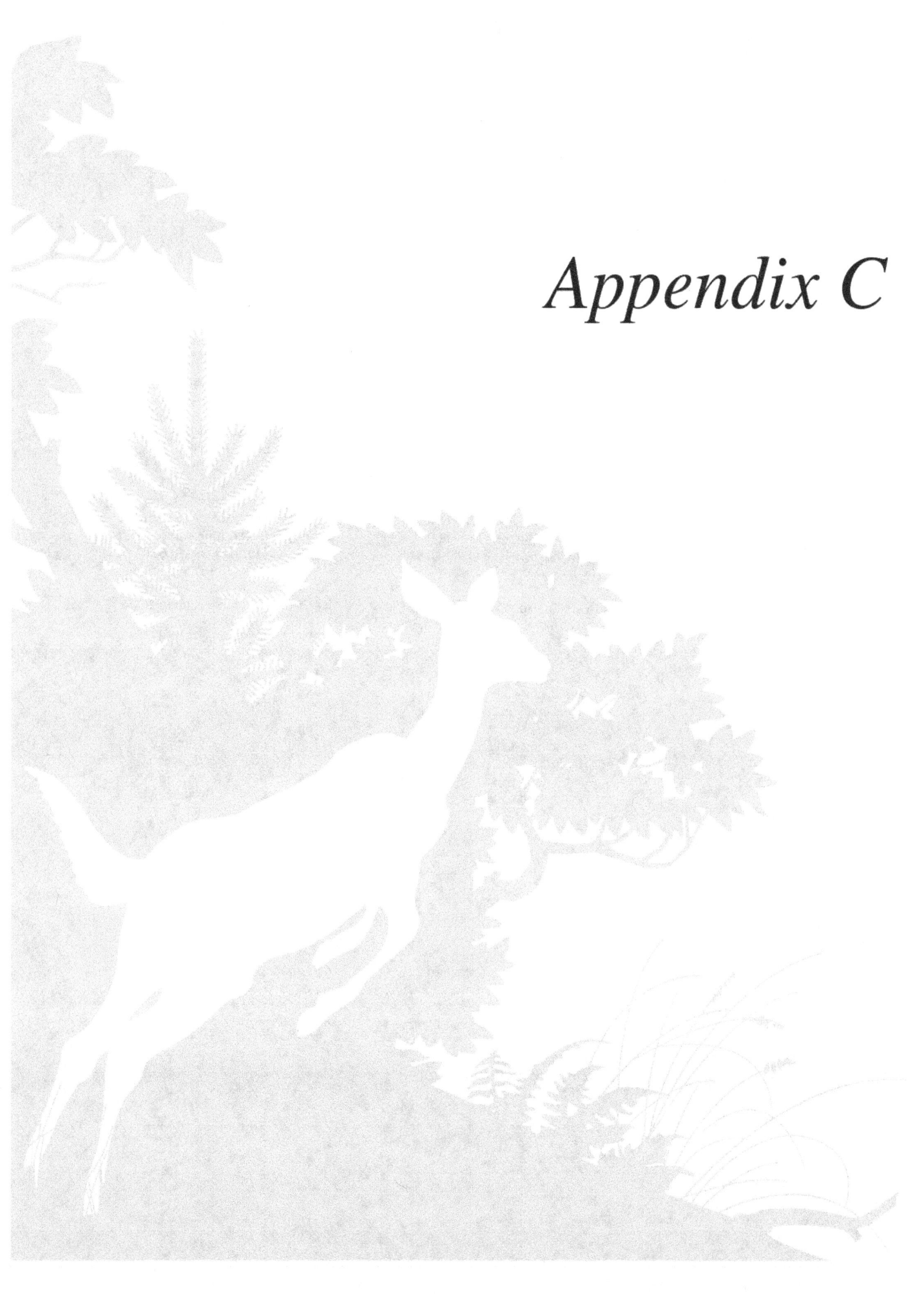

Appendix C

Appendix C.
Significant Methodological Changes From Previous Surveys and Regional Trends

This appendix provides a description of data collection changes and national and regional trend information based on the 1991, 1996, 2001, and 2006 Surveys. Since these four surveys used similar methodologies, their published information is directly comparable.

Significant Methodological Differences

The most significant design differences in the four surveys are as follows:

1. The 1991 Survey data were collected by interviewers filling out paper questionnaires. The data entries were keyed in a separate operation after the interview. The 1996, 2001, and 2006 Survey data were collected by the use of computer-assisted interviews. The questionnaires were programmed into computers, and the interviewer keyed in the responses at the time of the interview.

2. The 1991 Survey screening phase was conducted in January and February 1991, when the sample households were contacted and a household respondent was interviewed on behalf of the entire household. The screening interviews for the 1996, 2001, and 2006 Surveys were conducted April through June of their survey years in conjunction with the first wave of the detailed interviews. The screening interviews for all four surveys consisted primarily of demographic questions and wildlife-related recreation questions concerning activity in the previous year (1990, 1995, etc.) and intentions for recreating in the survey year.

In the 1991 Survey, an attempt was made to contact every sample person in all three detailed interview waves. In 1996, 2001, and 2006, respondents who were interviewed in the first detailed interview wave were not contacted again until the third wave. Also, all interviews in the second wave were conducted by telephone. In-person interviews were only conducted in the first and third waves.

Section I. Important Instrument Changes in the 1996 Survey

1. The 1991 Survey collected information on all wildlife-related recreation purchases made by participants without reference to where the purchase was made. The 1996 Survey asked in which state the purchase was made.

2. In 1991, respondents were asked what kind of fishing they did, i.e., Great Lakes, other freshwater, or saltwater, and then were asked in what states they fished. In 1996, respondents were asked in which states they fished and then were asked what kind of fishing they did. This method had the advantage of not asking about, for example, saltwater fishing when they only fished in a noncoastal state.

3. In 1991, respondents were asked how many days they "actually" hunted or fished for a particular type of game or fish and then how many days they "chiefly" hunted or fished for the same type of game or fish rather than another type of game or fish. To get total days of hunting or fishing for a particular type of game or fish, the "actually" day response was used, while to get the sum of all days of hunting or fishing, the "chiefly" days were summed. In 1996, respondents were asked their total days of hunting or fishing in the country and each state, then how many days

they hunted or fished for a particular type of game or fish.

4. Trip-related and equipment expenditure categories were not the same for all Surveys. "Guide fee" and "Pack trip or package fee" were two separate trip-related expenditure items in 1991, while they were combined into one category in the 1996 Survey. "Boating costs" was added to the 1996 hunting and wildlife-watching trip-related expenditure sections. "Heating and cooking fuel" was added to all of the trip-related expenditure sections. "Spearfishing equipment" was moved from a separate category to the "other" list. "Rods" and "Reels" were two separate categories in 1991 but were combined in 1996. "Lines, hooks, sinkers, etc." was one category in 1991 but split into "Lines" and "Hooks, sinkers, etc." in 1996. "Food used to feed other wildlife" was added to the wildlife-watching equipment section; "Boats" and "Cabins" were added to the wildlife-watching special equipment section; and "Land leasing and ownership" was added to the wildlife-watching expenditures section.

5. Questions asking sportspersons if they participated as much as they wanted were added in 1996. If the sportspersons said no, they were asked why not.

6. The 1991 Survey included questions about participation in organized fishing competitions; anglers using bows and arrows, nets or seines, or spearfishing; hunters using pistols or handguns and target shooting in preparation for hunting. These questions were not asked in 1996.

7. The 1996 Survey included questions about catch and release fishing and persons with disabilities participating in wildlife-related recreation. These questions were not part of the 1991 Survey.

8. The 1991 Survey included questions about average distance traveled to recreation sites. These questions were not included in the 1996 Survey.

9. The 1996 Survey included questions about the last trip the respondent took. Included were questions about the type of trip, where the activity took place, and the distance and direction to the site visited. These questions were not asked in 1991.

10. The 1991 Survey collected data on hunting, fishing, and wildlife watching by U.S. residents in Canada. The 1996 Survey collected data on fishing and wildlife watching by U.S. residents in Canada.

Section II. Important Instrument Changes in the 2001 Survey

1. The 1991 and 1996 single-race category "Asian or Pacific Islander" was changed to two categories "Asian" and "Native Hawaiian or Other Pacific Islander." In 1991 and 1996, the respondent was required to pick only one category, while in 2001 the respondent could pick any combination of categories. The next question stipulated that the respondent could only be identified with one category and then asked what that category was.

2. The 1991 and 1996 land leasing and ownership sections asked the respondent to combine the two types of land use into one and give total acreage and expenditures. In 2001, the two types of land use were explored separately.

3. The 1991 and 1996 wildlife-watching sections included questions on birdwatching for residential users only. The 2001 Survey added a question on birdwatching for nonresidential users. Also, questions on the use of birding life lists

and how many species the respondent can identify were added.

4. "Recreational vehicles" was added to the sportspersons and wildlife-watchers special equipment section. "House trailer" was added to the sportspersons special equipment section.

5. Total personal income was asked in the detailed phase of the 1996 Survey. This was changed to total household income in the 2001 Survey.

6. A question was added to the trip-related expenditures section to ascertain how much of the total was spent in the respondent's state of residence when the respondent participated in hunting, fishing, or wildlife watching out of state.

7. Boating questions were added to the fishing section. The respondent was asked about the extent of boat usage for the three types of fishing.

8. The 1996 Survey included questions about the months residential wildlife watchers fed birds. These questions were not repeated in the 2001 Survey.

9. The contingent valuation sections of the three types of wildlife-related recreation were altered, using an open-ended question format instead of the dichotomous choice format used in 1996.

Section III. Important Instrument Changes in the 2006 Survey

1. A series of boating questions was added. The new questions dealt with anglers using motorboats and/or non-motorboats, length of boat used most often, distance to boat launch used most often, needed improvements to facilities at the launch, whether or not the respondent completed a boating safety course, who the boater fished with most often, and the source and type of information the boater used for his or her fishing.

2. Questions regarding catch and release fishing were added. Whether or not the respondent

caught and released fish and, if so, the percent of fish released.

3. The proportion of hunting done with a rifle or shotgun, as contrasted with muzzleloader or archery equipment, was asked.

4. In the contingent valuation section, where the value of wildlife-related recreation was determined, two quality-variable questions were added: the average length of certain fish caught and whether a deer, elk, or moose was killed. Plus, the economic evaluation bid questions were rephrased, from "What is the most your [species] hunting in [State name] could have cost you per trip last year before you would NOT have gone [species] hunting at all in 2001, not even one trip, because it would have been too expensive?," for the hunters, for example, to "What is the cost that would have prevented you from taking even one such trip in 2006? In other words, if the trip cost was below this amount, you would have gone [species] hunting in [State name], but if the trip cost was above this amount, you would not have gone."

5. Questions concerning hunting, fishing, or wildlife watching in other countries were taken out of the Survey.

6. Questions about the reasons for not going hunting or fishing, or not going as much as expected, were deleted.

7. Disability of participants questions were taken out.

8. Determination of the types of sites for wildlife watching was discontinued.

9. The birding questions regarding the use of birding life lists and the ability to identify birds based on their sight or sounds were deleted.

10. Public transportation costs were divided into two sections, "public transportation by airplane" and "other public transportation, including trains, buses, and car rentals, etc."

National and Regional Trends

Fishing and Hunting

Comparing national hunting and fishing estimates for 1991 to 2006 finds participation declining over the entire time period. In 1991 and 1996, the number of people who hunted and fished remained essentially unchanged. In 2001, the number of sportspersons fell compared to the two previous survey estimates. In 2006, the number of anglers continued to decline and the number of hunters was stable.

The amount of time people spent fishing and hunting fluctuated between 1991 and 2006. The number of days spent fishing rose 22 percent between 1991 and 1996, fell 11 percent between 1996 and 2001, and fell 7 percent further between 2001 and 2006. Days of hunting followed a similar pattern. Between 1991 and 1996, hunting days increased 9 percent (although this increase was not statistically significant) but then fell 11 percent between 1996 and 2001 and a further 4 percent (this was not statistically significant either) between 2001 and 2006.

The amount of money spent for fishing and hunting trips and equipment rose from 1991 to 1996, fell from 1996 to 2001, and stayed level from 2001 to 2006. The comparisons are in constant dollars.

Wildlife Watching

There were differing trend lines from 1991 to 2006 for the two major types of wildlife watching. The number of overall wildlife watchers decreased 17 percent from 1991 to 1996, increased 5 percent from 1996 to 2001, and increased 8 percent from 2001 to 2006. Around-the-home wildlife watching, the most popular type of wildlife watching, led this trend with an 18 percent drop from 1991 to 1996, a 4 percent increase from 1996 to 2001, and an 8 percent increase from 2001 to 2006. Away-from-home wildlife watching, on the other hand, dropped from 1991 to 2001 (21 percent from 1991 to 1996 and 8 percent from 1996 to 2001) and stayed level with a statistically insignificant 5 percent increase from 2001 to 2006. Days afield by away-from-home wildlife watchers were significantly up from 1996 to 2001 and statistically stable the other time periods. Overall expenditures for wildlife watching increased 21 percent from 1991 to 1996 and 16 percent from 1996 to 2001 and decreased a statistically insignificant 7 percent from 2001 to 2006.

Table C-1a. Comparison of Wildlife-Related Recreation in the United States: 1991–1996

(U.S. population 16 years old and older. Numbers in thousands. All expenditures in 2006 dollars. 1996 expenditure categories made comparable to 1991)

Participants, days, and expenditures	1991 (Number)	1996 (Number)	1991–1996 percent change
Hunting			
Hunters, total	14,063	13,975	−1*
Hunting days, total.	235,806	256,676	9*
Hunting expenditures, total	$18,282,597	$26,224,069	43
Fishing			
Anglers, total	35,578	35,246	−1*
Fishing days, total	511,329	625,893	22
Fishing expenditures, total.	$35,553,365	$48,598,400	37
Wildlife Watching			
Wildlife watchers, total	76,111	62,868	−17
Around the home	73,904	60,751	−18
Away from home	29,999	23,652	−21
Wildlife-watching days, away from home	342,406	313,790	−8*
Wildlife-watching expenditures, total	$27,402,180	$33,093,660	21

* Not different from zero at the 5 percent level of significance.

Table C-1b. Comparison of Wildlife-Related Recreation in the United States: 1996–2001

(U.S. population 16 years old and older. Numbers in thousands. All expenditures in 2006 dollars. 1996 and 2001 expenditure categories made comparable to 1991)

Participants, days, and expenditures	1996 (Number)	2001 (Number)	1996–2001 percent change
Hunting			
Hunters, total	13,975	13,034	−7
Hunting days, total.	256,676	228,368	−11
Hunting expenditures, total	$26,224,069	$23,296,904	−11*
Fishing			
Anglers, total	35,246	34,071	−3
Fishing days, total	625,893	557,394	−11
Fishing expenditures, total.	$48,598,400	$40,399,711	−17
Wildlife Watching			
Wildlife watchers, total	62,868	66,105	5
Around the home	60,751	62,928	4
Away from home	23,652	21,823	−8
Wildlife-watching days, away from home	313,790	372,006	19
Wildlife-watching expenditures, total	$33,093,660	$38,453,190	16

* Not different from zero at the 5 percent level of significance.

Table C-1c. Comparison of Wildlife-Related Recreation in the United States: 2001–2006

(U.S. population 16 years old and older. Numbers in thousands. All expenditures in 2006 dollars. 2001 and 2006 expenditure categories made comparable to 1991)

Participants, days, and expenditures	2001 (Number)	2006 (Number)	2001–2006 percent change
Hunting			
Hunters, total	13,034	12,510	−4*
Hunting days, total....................................	228,368	219,925	−4*
Hunting expenditures, total	$23,296,904	$22,644,048	−3*
Fishing			
Anglers, total	34,071	29,952	−12
Fishing days, total	557,394	516,781	−7
Fishing expenditures, total..........................	$40,399,711	$42,042,188	4*
Wildlife Watching			
Wildlife watchers, total	66,105	71,132	8
Around the home....................................	62,928	67,756	8
Away from home....................................	21,823	22,977	5*
Wildlife-watching days, away from home	372,006	352,070	−5*
Wildlife-watching expenditures, total............................	$38,453,190	$35,870,403	−7*

* Not different from zero at the 5 percent level of significance.

Table C-1d. Comparison of Wildlife-Related Recreation in the United States: 1991–2006

(U.S. population 16 years old and older. Numbers in thousands. All expenditures in 2006 dollars. 2006 expenditure categories made comparable to 1991)

Participants, days, and expenditures	1991 (Number)	2006 (Number)	1991–2006 percent change
Hunting			
Hunters, total	14,063	12,510	−11
Hunting days, total....................................	235,806	219,925	−7*
Hunting expenditures, total	$18,282,597	$22,644,048	24
Fishing			
Anglers, total	35,578	29,952	−16
Fishing days, total	511,329	516,781	1*
Fishing expenditures, total..........................	$35,553,365	$42,042,188	18
Wildlife Watching			
Wildlife watchers, total	76,111	71,132	−7
Around the home....................................	73,904	67,756	−8
Away from home....................................	29,999	22,977	−23
Wildlife-watching days, away from home	342,406	352,070	3*
Wildlife-watching expenditures, total............................	$27,402,180	$35,870,403	31

* Not different from zero at the 5 percent level of significance.

Table C-2. Anglers and Hunters by Census Division: 1991, 1996, 2001, and 2006

(U.S. population 16 years old and older. Numbers in thousands)

Area and sportsperson	1991 Number	1991 Percent	1996 Number	1996 Percent	2001 Number	2001 Percent	2006 Number	2006 Percent
UNITED STATES								
Total population	189,964	100	201,472	100	212,298	100	229,245	100
Sportspersons	39,979	21	39,694	20	37,805	18	33,916	15
Anglers	35,578	19	35,246	17	34,067	16	29,952	13
Hunters	14,063	7	13,975	7	13,034	6	12,510	5
New England								
Total population	10,180	100	10,306	100	10,575	100	11,233	100
Sportspersons	1,658	16	1,673	16	1,504	14	1,353	12
Anglers	1,545	15	1,520	15	1,402	13	1,246	11
Hunters	444	4	465	5	386	4	374	3
Middle Atlantic								
Total population	29,216	100	29,371	100	29,806	100	31,518	100
Sportspersons	4,508	15	4,192	14	3,810	13	3,214	10
Anglers	3,871	13	3,627	12	3,250	11	2,550	8
Hunters	1,746	6	1,453	5	1,633	5	1,520	5
East North Central								
Total population	32,188	100	33,121	100	34,082	100	35,609	100
Sportspersons	7,202	22	6,912	21	6,400	19	5,975	17
Anglers	6,264	19	6,006	18	5,655	17	5,190	15
Hunters	2,789	9	2,712	8	2,421	7	2,376	7
West North Central								
Total population	13,504	100	13,875	100	14,430	100	15,458	100
Sportspersons	4,143	31	3,977	29	4,239	29	3,836	25
Anglers	3,647	27	3,416	25	3,836	27	3,284	21
Hunters	1,709	13	1,917	14	1,710	12	1,779	12
South Atlantic								
Total population	33,682	100	36,776	100	39,286	100	43,965	100
Sportspersons	6,996	21	7,282	20	6,957	18	6,633	15
Anglers	6,441	19	6,636	18	6,451	16	6,116	14
Hunters	2,083	6	2,050	6	1,875	5	1,884	4
East South Central								
Total population	11,667	100	12,459	100	12,976	100	13,722	100
Sportspersons	2,984	26	2,907	23	2,865	22	2,689	20
Anglers	2,635	23	2,514	20	2,543	20	2,436	18
Hunters	1,279	11	1,301	10	1,164	9	1,101	8
West South Central								
Total population	19,926	100	21,811	100	23,337	100	25,407	100
Sportspersons	5,125	26	5,093	23	4,924	21	4,499	18
Anglers	4,592	23	4,616	21	4,375	19	3,952	16
Hunters	1,843	9	1,812	8	1,988	9	1,810	7
Mountain								
Total population	10,092	100	11,966	100	13,308	100	15,651	100
Sportspersons	2,488	25	2,761	23	2,757	21	2,372	15
Anglers	2,079	21	2,411	20	2,443	18	2,084	13
Hunters	1,069	11	1,061	9	1,020	8	868	6
Pacific								
Total population	29,508	100	31,787	100	34,498	100	36,681	100
Sportspersons	4,875	17	4,897	15	4,349	13	3,345	9
Anglers	4,505	15	4,501	14	4,111	12	3,094	8
Hunters	1,101	4	1,203	4	837	2	798	2

Table C-3. Wildlife Watching Participants by Census Division: 1991, 1996, 2001, and 2006

(Numbers in thousands. Population 16 years old and older)

Area and wildlife watcher	1991		1996		2001		2006	
	Number	Percent	Number	Percent	Number	Percent	Number	Percent
UNITED STATES								
Total population	189,964	100	201,472	100	212,298	100	229,245	100
Total wildlife watchers	76,111	40	62,868	31	66,105	31	71,132	31
Away from home	29,999	16	23,652	12	21,823	10	22,977	10
Around the home	73,904	39	60,751	30	62,928	30	67,756	30
New England								
Total population	10,180	100	10,306	100	10,575	100	11,233	100
Total wildlife watchers	4,598	45	3,710	36	3,875	37	4,489	40
Away from home	1,856	18	1,443	14	1,155	11	1,340	12
Around the home	4,544	45	3,586	35	3,765	36	4,310	38
Middle Atlantic								
Total population	29,216	100	29,371	100	29,806	100	31,518	100
Total wildlife watchers	10,556	36	8,185	28	8,740	29	8,723	28
Away from home	4,166	14	2,960	10	2,849	10	2,729	9
Around the home	10,282	35	8,023	27	8,452	28	8,451	27
East North Central								
Total population	32,188	100	33,121	100	34,082	100	35,609	100
Total wildlife watchers	14,511	45	11,731	35	11,631	34	12,215	34
Away from home	5,572	17	4,501	14	3,571	10	3,792	11
Around the home	14,175	44	11,297	34	11,196	33	11,845	33
West North Central								
Total population	13,504	100	13,875	100	14,430	100	15,458	100
Total wildlife watchers	6,924	51	5,089	37	6,206	43	6,741	44
Away from home	2,654	20	1,927	14	2,059	14	2,163	14
Around the home	6,722	50	4,900	35	5,938	41	6,447	42
South Atlantic								
Total population	33,682	100	36,776	100	39,286	100	43,965	100
Total wildlife watchers	13,047	39	11,252	31	11,395	29	12,862	29
Away from home	4,450	13	3,992	11	3,469	9	3,208	7
Around the home	12,813	38	10,964	30	10,911	28	12,432	28
East South Central								
Total population	11,667	100	12,459	100	12,976	100	13,722	100
Total wildlife watchers	4,864	42	3,904	31	4,514	35	4,931	36
Away from home	1,592	14	1,118	9	1,086	8	1,758	13
Around the home	4,765	41	3,795	30	4,390	34	4,683	34
West South Central								
Total population	19,926	100	21,811	100	23,337	100	25,407	100
Total wildlife watchers	7,035	35	5,933	27	5,747	25	6,764	27
Away from home	2,459	12	2,096	10	1,822	8	2,127	8
Around the home	6,817	34	5,773	26	5,490	24	6,319	25
Mountain								
Total population	10,092	100	11,966	100	13,308	100	15,651	100
Total wildlife watchers	4,437	44	4,099	34	4,619	35	4,968	32
Away from home	2,215	22	1,967	16	2,019	15	2,004	13
Around the home	4,145	41	3,855	32	4,282	32	4,605	29
Pacific								
Total population	29,508	100	31,787	100	34,498	100	36,681	100
Total wildlife watchers	10,139	34	8,966	28	9,377	27	9,439	26
Away from home	5,035	17	3,648	11	3,793	11	3,856	11
Around the home	9,641	33	8,558	27	8,504	25	8,664	24

Appendix D

Appendix D.
Sample Design and Statistical Accuracy

This appendix is presented in two parts. The first part is the U.S. Census Bureau Source and Accuracy Statement. This statement describes the sampling design for the 2006 Survey and highlights the steps taken to produce estimates from the completed questionnaires. The statement explains the use of standard errors and confidence intervals. It also provides comprehensive information about errors characteristic of surveys and formulas and parameters to calculate an approximate standard error or confidence interval for each number published in this report. The second part reports approximate standard errors for selected measures of participation and expenditures for wildlife-related recreation. Tables D-1 to D-3 show common estimates by state with their estimated standard errors. Tables D-4 to D-9 provide parameters for computing standard errors.

Source and Accuracy Statement for the Alabama State Report of the *2006 National Survey of Fishing, Hunting, and Wildlife-Associated Recreation*

SOURCE OF DATA

The estimates in this report are based on data collected in the *2006 National Survey of Fishing, Hunting, and Wildlife-Associated Recreation* (FHWAR) conducted by the Census Bureau and sponsored by the U.S. Fish and Wildlife Service.

The eligible universe for the FHWAR is the civilian noninstitutionalized and nonbarrack military population living in the United States. The institutionalized population, which is excluded from the population universe, is composed primarily of the population in correctional institutions and nursing homes (91 percent of the 4.1 million institutionalized people in Census 2000).

The 2006 Survey was designed to provide state-level estimates of the number of participants in recreational hunting and fishing and in wildlife-watching activities (e.g., wildlife observation). Information was collected on the number of participants, where and how often they participated, the type of wildlife encountered, and the amounts of money spent on wildlife-related recreation.

The Survey was conducted in two stages: an initial screening of households to identify likely sportspersons and wildlife-watching participants and a series of follow-up interviews of selected persons to collect detailed data about their wildlife-related recreation during 2006.

SAMPLE DESIGN

The 2006 FHWAR sample was selected from the Census Bureau's master address file (MAF) and unused sample of the Current Population Survey (CPS). The CPS sample was used to improve coverage in rural areas of some states.

The FHWAR is a multistage probability sample, with coverage in all 50 states and the District of Columbia. In the first stage of the sampling process, primary sampling units (PSUs) are selected for sample. The PSUs are defined to correspond to the Office of Management and Budget definitions of Core Based Statistical Area definitions and to improve efficiency in field operations. The United States is divided into 2,025 PSUs. These PSUs are grouped into 824 strata. Within each stratum, a single PSU is chosen for the sample, with its probability of selection proportional to its population as of the most recent decennial census. This PSU represents the entire stratum from which it was selected. In the case of strata consisting of only one PSU, the PSU is chosen with certainty.

Within the selected PSUs, the FHWAR sample was selected from the MAF where sufficient coverage of addresses existed. In some rural areas, the sample was selected from unused cases from the CPS to improve coverage.

FHWAR Screening Sample

The total screening sample in Alabama consisted of **1,522** households. Interviewing for the screen was conducted during April, May, and June 2006. Of all housing units in sample, about **1,264** were determined to be eligible for interview. Interviewers obtained interviews at **1,211** of these units for a state response rate of **96** percent. Local field representatives conducted interviews by telephone when possible, otherwise through a personal visit. The field representatives asked screening questions for all household members 6 years old and older. Noninterviews occur when the occupants are not found at home after repeated calls or are unavailable for some other reason.

Data for the FHWAR sportspersons sample and wildlife-watchers sample were collected in three waves. The first wave started in April 2006, the second in September 2006, and the third in January 2007. In the sportspersons sample, all persons who hunted or fished in 2006 by the time of the screening interview were interviewed in the first wave. The remaining sportspersons in sample were interviewed in the second wave. A subsampling operation was conducted before the third wave of sampling to reduce cost of the Survey, and everyone remaining in sample was interviewed in the third wave.

The reference period was the preceding 4 months for waves 1 and 2. In wave 3, the reference period was either 4, 8, or 12 months depending on when the sample person was first interviewed.

Detailed Samples

Two independent detailed samples were chosen from the FHWAR screening sample. One consisted of sportspersons (people who hunt or fish) and the other of wildlife watchers (people who observe, photograph, or feed wildlife).

A. Sportspersons

The Census Bureau selected the detailed samples based on information reported during the screening phase. Based on information collected from the household respondent, every person 16 years old and older in the FHWAR screening sample was assigned to a sportspersons stratum. The criteria for the strata included time devoted to hunting or fishing in previous years, participation in hunting or fishing in 2006 by the time of the screening interview, and intentions to participate in hunting and fishing activities during the remainder of 2006. The four sportspersons categories were:

1. *Active*—a person who had already participated in hunting or fishing in 2006 at the time of the screener interview.

2. *Likely*—a person who had not participated in 2006 at the time of the screener, but had participated in 2005 OR was likely to participate in 2006.

3. *Inactive*—a person who had not participated in 2005 or 2006 AND was somewhat unlikely to participate in 2006.

4. *Nonparticipant*—a person who had not participated in 2005 or 2006 AND was very unlikely to participate in 2006.

Persons were selected for the detailed phase based on these groupings.

Active sportspersons were given the detailed interview twice—at the time of the screening interview (in April, May, or June 2006) and again in January or February 2007. Likely sportspersons and a subsample of the inactive sportspersons were also interviewed twice—first in September or October 2006,

then in January or February 2007. If Census Bureau field representatives were not able to obtain the first interview, they attempted to interview the person in the final interviewing period with the reference period being the entire year. Persons in the nonparticipant group were not eligible for a detailed interview.

About **620** persons were designated for interviews in Alabama. The detailed sportspersons sample sizes varied by state to get reliable state-level estimates. During each interview period, about **19** percent of the designated persons were not found at home or were unavailable for some other reason. Overall, about **501** detailed sportspersons interviews were completed at a response rate of **81** percent.

B. Wildlife Watchers

The wildlife-watching detailed sample was also selected based on information reported during the screening phase. Based on information collected from the household respondent, every person 16 years old and older was assigned to a stratum. The criteria for the strata included time devoted to wildlife-watching activities in previous years, participation in wildlife-watching activities in 2006 by the time of the screening interview, and intentions to participate in wildlife-watching activities during the remainder of 2006. The five wildlife-watching categories were:

1. *Active*—a person who had already participated in 2006 at the time of the screening interview.

2. *Avid*—a person who had not yet participated in 2006, but in 2005 had taken trips to participate in wildlife-watching activities for 21 or more days or had spent $300 or more.

3. *Average*—a person who had not yet participated in 2006, but in 2005 had taken trips to wildlife watch for less than 21 days and had spent less than $300 OR had not participated in wildlife-watching activities but was very

likely to in the remainder of 2006.

4. *Infrequent*—a person who had not participated in 2005 or 2006, but was somewhat likely or somewhat unlikely to participate in the remainder of 2006.

5. *Nonparticipant*—a person who had not participated in 2005 or 2006 AND was very unlikely to participate during the remainder of 2006.

Persons were selected for the detailed sample based on these groupings, but persons in the nonparticipant group were not eligible for a detailed interview. A subsample of each of the other groups was selected to receive a detailed interview with the chance of selection diminishing as the likelihood of participation diminished.

Wildlife-watching participants were given the detailed interview twice. Some received their first detailed interview at the same time as the screening interview (in April, May, or June 2006). The rest received their first detailed interview in September or October 2006. All wildlife-watching participants received their second interview in January or February 2007. If Census Bureau field representatives were not able to obtain the first interview, they attempted to interview the person in the final interviewing period with the reference period being the entire year.

About **191** persons were designated for interviews in Alabama. The detailed wildlife-watching sample sizes varied by state to get reliable state-level estimates. During each interview period, about **20** percent of the designated persons were not found at home or were unavailable for some other reason. Overall, about **153** detailed wildlife-watcher interviews were completed at a response rate of **80** percent.

ESTIMATION PROCEDURE

Several stages of adjustments were used to derive the final 2006 FHWAR person weights. A brief description of the major components of the weights is given next.

All statistics for the population 6 to 15 years of age were derived from the screening interview. Statistics for the population 16 years old and older come from both the screening and detailed interviews. Estimates that come from the screening sample are presented in Appendix B.

A. Screening Sample

Every interviewed person in the screening sample received a screening weight that was the product of the following factors:

1. *Base Weight.* The base weight is the inverse of the household's probability of selection.

2. *Household Noninterview Adjustment.* The noninterview adjustment inflates the weight assigned to interviewed households to account for households eligible for interview but for which no interview was obtained.

3. *First-Stage Adjustment.* The 824 areas designated for our samples were selected from 2,025 such areas of the United States. Some sample areas represent only themselves and are referred to as self-representing. The remaining areas represent other areas similar in selected characteristics and are thus designated non-self-representing. The first-stage factor reduces the component of variation arising from sampling the non-self-representing areas.

4. *Second-Stage Adjustment.* This adjustment brings the estimates of the total population into agreement with census-based estimates of the civilian noninstitutionalized and nonbarrack military populations for each state.

B. Sportspersons Sample

Every interviewed person in the sportspersons detailed sample received a weight that was the product of the following factors:

1. *Screening Weight.* This is the person's final weight from the screening sample.

2. *Sportspersons Stratum Adjustment.* This factor inflates the weights of persons selected for the detailed sample to account for the subsampling done within each sportsperson stratum.

3. *Sportspersons Noninterview Adjustment.* This factor adjusts the weights of the interviewed sportspersons to account for sportspersons selected for the detailed sample for whom no interview was obtained. A person was considered a noninterview if he or she was not interviewed in the third wave of interviewing.

4. *Sportspersons Ratio Adjustment Factor.* This is a ratio adjustment of the detailed sample to the screening sample within the sportspersons sampling stratum. This adjustment brings the population estimates of persons aged 16 years old and older from the detailed sample into agreement with the same estimates from the screening sample, which was a much larger sample.

C. Wildlife-Watchers Sample

Every interviewed person in the wildlife-watchers detailed sample received a weight that was the product of the following factors:

1. *Screening Weight.* This is the person's final weight from the screening sample.

2. *Wildlife-Watchers Stratum Adjustment.* This factor inflates the weights of persons selected for the detailed sample to account for the subsampling done within each wildlife-watcher stratum.

3. *Wildlife-Watchers Noninterview Adjustment.* This factor adjusts the weights of the interviewed wildlife-watching participants to account for wildlife watchers selected for the detailed sample for which no interview was obtained. A person was considered a noninterview if he or she was not interviewed in the third wave of interviewing.

4. *Wildlife-Watchers Ratio Adjustment Factor.* This is a ratio adjustment of the detailed sample to the screening sample within wildlife-watchers sampling strata. This adjustment brings the population estimates of persons aged 16 years old and older from the detailed sample into agreement with the same estimates from the screening sample, which was a much larger sample.

ACCURACY OF THE ESTIMATES

A sample survey estimate has two types of error: sampling and nonsampling. The accuracy of an estimate depends on both types of error. The nature of the sampling error is known given the survey design; the full extent of the nonsampling error is unknown.

NONSAMPLING ERROR

For a given estimator, the difference between the estimate that would result if the sample were to include the entire population and the true population value being estimated is known as nonsampling error. There are several sources of nonsampling error that may occur during the development or execution of the survey. It can occur because of circumstances created by the interviewer, the respondent, the survey instrument, or the way the data are collected and processed. For example, errors could occur because:

- The interviewer records the wrong answer, the respondent provides incorrect information, the respondent estimates the requested information, or an unclear survey question is misunderstood by the respondent (measurement error).

- Some individuals who should have been included in the survey frame were missed (coverage error).

- Responses are not collected from all those in the sample or the respondent is unwilling to provide information (nonresponse error).

- Values are estimated imprecisely for missing data (imputation error).

- Forms may be lost, data may be incorrectly keyed, coded, or recoded, etc. (processing error).

The Census Bureau employs quality control procedures throughout the production process, including the overall design of surveys, the wording of questions, the review of the work of interviewers and coders, and the statistical review of reports to minimize these errors.

Two types of nonsampling error that can be examined to a limited extent are nonresponse and undercoverage.

Nonresponse. The effect of nonresponse cannot be measured directly, but one indication of its potential effect is the nonresponse rate. For the FHWAR screener interview in Alabama, the household-level nonresponse rate was 4 percent. The person-level nonresponse rate for the detailed sportsperson interview in Alabama was an additional 19 percent and for the wildlife watchers it was 20 percent. Since the screener nonresponse rate is a household-level rate and the detailed interview nonresponse rate is a person-level rate, we cannot combine these rates to derive an overall nonresponse rate. Since it is unlikely the nonresponding households to the FHWAR have the same number of persons as the households successfully interviewed, combining these rates would result in an overestimate of the "true" person-level overall nonresponse rate for the detailed interviews.

Coverage. Overall screener undercoverage is estimated to be about 13 percent. Ratio estimation to independent population controls, as described previously, partially corrects for the bias due to survey undercoverage. However, biases exist in the estimates to the extent that missed persons in missed households or missed persons in interviewed households have different characteristics from those of interviewed persons in the same age group.

Comparability of Data. Data obtained from the 2006 FHWAR and other sources are not entirely comparable. This results from differences in interviewer training and experience and in differing survey processes. This is an example of nonsampling variability not reflected in the standard errors. Therefore, caution should be used when comparing results from different sources. (See Appendix C.)

A Nonsampling Error Warning. Since the full extent of the nonsampling error is unknown, one should be particularly careful when interpreting results based on small differences between estimates. The Census Bureau recommends that data users incorporate information about nonsampling errors into their analyses, as nonsampling error could impact the conclusions drawn from the results. Caution should also be used when interpreting results based on a relatively small number of cases. Summary measures (such as medians and percentage distributions) probably do not reveal useful information when computed on a subpopulation smaller than 50,000 for screener data, 65,000 for the detailed sportsperson data, and 230,000 for the wildlife-watchers data.

SAMPLING ERROR

Since the FHWAR estimates come from a sample, they may differ from figures from an enumeration of the entire population using the same questionnaires, instructions, and enumerators. For a given estimator, the difference between an estimate based on a sample and the estimate that would result if the sample were to include the entire population is known as sampling error. Standard errors, as calculated by methods described in "Standard Errors and Their Use," are primarily measures of the magnitude of sampling error. However, they may include some nonsampling error.

Standard Errors and Their Use. The sample estimate and its standard error enable one to construct a confidence interval. A confidence interval is a range that has a known probability of including the average result of all possible samples. For example, if all possible samples were surveyed under essentially the same general conditions and using the same sample design, and if an estimate and its standard error were calculated from each sample, then approximately 90 percent of the intervals from 1.645 standard errors below the estimate to 1.645 standard errors above the estimate would include the average result of all possible samples.

A particular confidence interval may or may not contain the average estimate derived from all possible samples. However, one can say with specified confidence that the interval includes the average estimate calculated from all possible samples.

Standard errors may also be used to perform hypothesis testing, a procedure for distinguishing between population parameters using sample estimates. The most common type of hypothesis is that the population parameters are different. An example would be comparing the proportion of anglers to the proportion of hunters.

Tests may be performed at various levels of significance. A significance level is the probability of concluding that the characteristics are different when, in fact, they are the same. For example, to conclude that two characteristics are different at the 0.1 level of significance, the absolute value of the estimated difference between characteristics must be greater than or equal to 1.645 times the standard error of the difference.

This report uses 90-percent confidence intervals and 0.1 level of significance to determine statistical validity. Consult standard statistical textbooks for alternative criteria.

Estimating Standard Errors. The Census Bureau uses replication methods to estimate the standard errors of FHWAR estimates. These methods primarily measure the magnitude of sampling error. However, they do measure some effects of nonsampling error as well. They do not measure systematic biases in the data associated with nonsampling error. Bias is the average over all possible samples of the differences between the sample estimates and the true value.

Generalized Variance Parameters. While it is possible to compute and present an estimate of the standard error based on the survey data for each estimate in a report, there are a number of reasons why this is not done. A presentation of the individual standard errors would be of limited use, since one could not possibly predict all of the combinations of results that may be of interest to data users. Additionally, data users have access to FHWAR microdata files, and it is impossible to compute in advance the standard error for every estimate one might obtain from those data sets. Moreover, variance estimates are based on sample data and have variances of their own. Therefore, some methods of stabilizing these estimates of variance, for example, by generalizing or averaging over time, may be used to improve their reliability.

Experience has shown that certain groups of estimates have similar relationships between their variances and expected values. Modeling or generalizing may provide more stable variance estimates by taking advantage of these similarities. The generalized variance function is a simple model that expresses the variance as a function of the expected value of the survey estimate. The parameters of the generalized variance function are estimated using direct replicate variances. These generalized variance parameters provide a relatively easy method to obtain approximate standard errors for numerous characteristics. Tables D-4 to D-9 provide the generalized variance parameters for FHWAR data. Methods for using the parameters to calculate standard errors of various estimates are given in the next sections.

Standard Errors of Estimated Numbers. The approximate standard error, s_x, of an estimated number shown in this report can be obtained using the following formulas. Formula (1) is used to calculate the standard errors of levels of sportspersons, anglers, and wildlife watchers.

$$s_x = \sqrt{ax^2 + bx} \qquad (1)$$

Here, x is the size of the estimate and a and b are the parameters in the tables associated with the particular characteristic.

Formula (2) is used for standard errors of aggregates, i.e., trips, days, and expenditures.

$$s_x = \sqrt{ax^2 + bx + \frac{cx^2}{y}} \qquad (2)$$

Here, x is again the size of the estimate; y is the base of the estimate; and a, b, and c are the parameters in the tables associated with the particular characteristic.

Illustration of the Computation of the Standard Error of an Estimated Number

Suppose there were an estimated 33,916,000 persons age 16 years old and older who either fished or hunted in the United States in 2006. Using formula (1) with the parameters a = –0.000027 and b = 6,125 from table D-5, the approximate standard error of the estimated number of 33,916,000 sportspersons age 16 years old and older is

$$s_x = \sqrt{-0.000027 \times 33,916,000^2 + 6,125 \times 33,916,000} = 420,330$$

The 90-percent confidence interval for the estimated number of sportspersons 16 years old and older is from 33,225,000 to 34,607,000, i.e., 33,916,000 ± 1.645 x 420,330. Therefore, a conclusion that the average estimate derived from all possible samples lies within a range computed in this way would be correct for roughly 90 percent of all possible samples.

Suppose there were an estimated 12,510,000 hunters aged 16 years old and older who engaged in 219,925,000 days of participation in 2006. Using formula (2) with the parameters a = –0.000235, b = –85,241, and c = 22,698 from table D-7, the approximate standard error on 219,925,000 estimated days on an estimated base of 12,510,000 hunters is

$$s_x = \sqrt{-0.000235 \times 219,925,000^2 - 85,241 \times 219,925,000 + \frac{22,698 \times 219,925,000^2}{12,510,000}} = 7,592,000$$

The 90-percent confidence interval on the estimate of 219,925,000 days is from 207,436,000 to 232,414,000, i.e., 219,925,000 ± 1.645 x 7,592,000. Again, a conclusion that the average estimate derived from all possible samples lies within a range computed in this way would be correct for roughly 90 percent of all possible samples.

Standard Errors of Estimated Percentages. The reliability of an estimated percentage, computed using sample data for both numerator and denominator, depends on the size of the percentage and its base. Estimated percentages are relatively more reliable than the corresponding estimates of the numerators of the percentages, particularly if the percentages are 50 percent or more. When the numerator and the denominator of the percentage are in different categories, use the parameter in the tables indicated by the numerator.

The approximate standard error, $s_{x,p}$, can be obtained by use of the formula

$$s_{x,p} = \sqrt{\frac{bp(100 - p)}{x}} \qquad (3)$$

Here, x is the total number of sportspersons, hunters, etc., which is the base of the percentage; p is the percentage $(0 \le p \le 100)$; and b is the parameter in the tables associated with the characteristic in the numerator of the percentage.

Illustration of the Computation of the Standard Error of an Estimated Percentage

Suppose there were an estimated 12,510,000 hunters aged 16 years old and older of whom 18.3 percent hunted migratory birds. From table D-5, the appropriate b parameter is 5,756. Using formula (3), the approximate standard error on the estimate of 18.3 percent is

$$s_{x,p} = \sqrt{\frac{5,756 \times 18.3 \times (100 - 18.3)}{12,510,000}} = 0.83$$

Consequently, the 90-percent confidence interval for the estimate percentage of migratory bird hunters 16 years old and older is from 16.9 percent to 19.7 percent, i.e., $18.3 \pm 1.645 \times 0.83$.

Standard Error of a Difference. The standard error of the difference between two sample estimates is approximately equal to

$$s_{x-y} = \sqrt{s_x^2 + s_y^2} \tag{4}$$

where s_x and s_y are the standard errors of the estimates x and y. The estimates can be numbers, percentages, ratios, etc. This will represent the actual standard error quite accurately for the difference between estimates of the same characteristic in two different areas, or for the difference between separate and uncorrelated characteristics in the same area. However, if there is a high positive (negative) correlation between the two characteristics, the formula will overestimate (underestimate) the true standard error.

Illustration of the Computation of the Standard Error of a Difference

Suppose there were an estimated 11,655,000 females in the age range of 18 to 24 of whom 726,000 or 6.2 percent were sportspersons. Similarly, suppose there were an estimated 11,638,000 males in the same age range of whom 1,929,000 or 16.6 percent were sportspersons. The apparent difference between the percentage of female and male sportspersons is 10.4 percent. Using formula (3) and the appropriate b parameter from table D-5, the approximate standard errors of 6.2 percent and 16.6 percent are 0.55 and 0.85, respectively. Using formula (4), the approximate standard error of the estimated difference of 10.4 percent is

$$s_{x-y} = \sqrt{0.55^2 + 0.85^2} = 1.02$$

The 90-percent confidence interval on the difference between 18-to-24-year-old female and male sportspersons is from 8.7 to 12.1, i.e., $10.4 \pm 1.645 \times 1.02$. Since the interval does not contain zero, we can conclude with 90-percent confidence that the percentage of 18-to-24-year-old female sportspersons is less than the percentage of 18-to-24-year-old male sportspersons.

Standard Errors of Estimated Averages. Certain mean values for sportspersons, anglers, etc., shown in the report were calculated as the ratio of two numbers. For example, average days per angler is calculated as:

$$\frac{x}{y} = \frac{total\ days}{total\ anglers}$$

Standard errors for these averages may be approximated by the use of formula (5) below.

$$s_{x/y} = \frac{x}{y}\sqrt{\left[\frac{s_x}{x}\right]^2 + \left[\frac{s_y}{y}\right]^2 - 2r\frac{s_x s_y}{xy}} \tag{5}$$

In formula (5), r represents the correlation coefficient between the numerator and the denominator of the estimate. In the above formula, use 0.7 as an estimate of r.

Illustration of the Computation of the Standard Error of an Estimated Average

Suppose that the estimated number of the average days per angler aged 16 years old and older for all fishing was 17.3 days. Using formulas (1) and (2) above, we compute the standard error on total days, 516,781,000, and total anglers, 29,952,000, to be 15,828,079 and 399,342, respectively. The approximate standard error on the estimated average of 17.3 days is

$$
S_{x/y} = \frac{516,781,000}{29,952,000} \sqrt{\left[\frac{158,280,079}{516,781,000}\right]^2 + \left[\frac{399,342}{29,952,000}\right]^2 - 2 \times 0.7 \frac{15,828,079 \times 399,342}{516,781,000 \times 29,952,000}} = 0.40
$$

Therefore, the 90-percent confidence interval on the estimated average of 17.3 days is from 16.6 to 18.0, i.e., $17.3 \pm 1.645 \times 0.40$.

Table D-1. **Approximate Standard Errors of Resident Anglers, Days of Fishing by State Residents, and Expenditures for Fishing by State Residents**

(Numbers in thousands)

State	Participation		Days		Expenditures in dollars	
	Estimate	Standard error	Estimate	Standard error	Estimate	Standard error
Alabama	628	41	13,164	2,463	791,187	136,335
Alaska	138	10	1,965	329	221,328	43,350
Arizona	370	32	4,378	1,163	293,510	62,037
Arkansas	463	38	10,078	1,788	364,528	71,945
California	1,689	102	19,649	2,646	2,707,995	428,592
Colorado	554	40	6,737	1,081	1,093,571	147,080
Connecticut	291	20	6,239	1,239	442,724	95,897
Delaware	76	6	1,521	397	138,601	28,408
Florida	1,950	100	43,026	5,370	3,618,499	514,463
Georgia	1,060	77	18,449	3,935	1,050,608	183,960
Hawaii	94	8	1,345	300	82,728	22,551
Idaho	223	22	4,126	1,222	234,363	52,127
Illinois	1,034	62	21,351	2,579	1,315,192	197,171
Indiana	739	50	10,583	1,315	696,389	128,034
Iowa	449	34	7,017	1,319	398,654	78,100
Kansas	369	27	5,643	916	299,896	63,027
Kentucky	622	45	9,874	1,600	963,254	239,107
Louisiana	598	47	11,075	1,337	807,063	153,792
Maine	225	17	3,854	800	147,473	26,410
Maryland	475	32	6,571	1,028	661,078	99,475
Massachusetts	452	29	9,309	1,784	954,647	229,603
Michigan	1,098	89	23,239	4,004	1,662,875	364,329
Minnesota	1,143	75	23,025	4,850	2,467,491	483,774
Mississippi	479	34	7,515	1,198	280,529	55,307
Missouri	931	59	16,227	2,889	1,032,407	160,090
Montana	179	16	2,455	424	140,895	27,916
Nebraska	192	15	3,208	532	217,437	36,020
Nevada	156	16	1,958	447	304,133	73,096
New Hampshire	124	10	2,488	442	141,041	27,264
New Jersey	530	33	9,237	1,601	1,167,944	196,789
New Mexico	190	18	2,451	838	254,023	76,563
New York	1,029	81	16,157	3,315	844,153	194,665
North Carolina	964	63	16,106	2,626	1,039,286	198,626
North Dakota	106	8	1,150	205	96,908	19,580
Ohio	1,293	91	17,583	3,199	1,118,439	226,342
Oklahoma	547	39	10,363	1,487	486,013	88,047
Oregon	483	39	8,104	2,308	507,625	101,717
Pennsylvania	990	87	20,592	4,258	1,625,022	272,116
Rhode Island	83	6	1,480	207	125,121	25,668
South Carolina	548	39	11,174	1,814	1,101,128	340,271
South Dakota	95	9	1,456	254	137,159	28,262
Tennessee	708	54	13,966	2,025	576,667	110,670
Texas	2,344	172	40,101	5,924	3,883,589	796,872
Utah	313	26	3,841	851	408,986	84,433
Vermont	71	7	1,506	279	59,132	12,200
Virginia	731	58	9,932	1,331	669,565	140,722
Washington	690	43	9,111	1,394	967,520	180,668
West Virginia	306	25	6,967	1,000	335,880	104,458
Wisconsin	1,025	66	17,771	2,431	1,193,390	201,965
Wyoming	98	10	1,360	282	450,339	133,641

Table D-2. Approximate Standard Errors of Resident Hunters, Days of Hunting by State Residents, and Expenditures for Hunting by State Residents

(Numbers in thousands)

State	Participation		Days		Expenditures in dollars	
	Estimate	Standard error	Estimate	Standard error	Estimate	Standard error
Alabama	312	30	8,032	1,831	596,485	114,760
Alaska	55	7	859	205	111,535	25,306
Arizona	129	15	1,535	405	360,537	108,628
Arkansas	307	31	7,630	1,629	765,599	146,698
California	317	43	4,192	1,041	960,932	230,698
Colorado	132	18	1,421	303	219,545	57,088
Connecticut	40	7	693	181	96,638	38,704
Delaware	21	3	512	148	33,836	7,761
Florida	325	40	5,723	1,200	870,391	205,731
Georgia	356	42	7,180	1,643	502,017	135,282
Hawaii	19	4	421	214	24,992	9,869
Idaho	123	15	1,187	256	142,708	33,385
Illinois	272	32	4,609	938	416,950	80,383
Indiana	254	30	4,617	930	243,058	60,232
Iowa	210	26	3,734	869	260,147	60,083
Kansas	192	23	2,717	723	231,228	58,822
Kentucky	261	29	5,108	637	507,473	116,274
Louisiana	275	33	7,155	1,443	618,264	142,285
Maine	146	14	2,042	319	211,434	40,017
Maryland	151	17	2,213	399	230,214	44,830
Massachusetts	66	11	1,629	562	238,670	98,246
Michigan	721	79	11,756	2,256	846,455	202,158
Minnesota	536	53	6,947	1,571	752,098	171,270
Mississippi	244	24	6,227	820	446,639	89,602
Missouri	560	49	9,685	1,876	1,027,698	167,223
Montana	145	14	1,817	315	219,465	46,679
Nebraska	105	13	1,647	349	176,456	33,615
Nevada	60	10	687	249	149,750	51,854
New Hampshire	52	6	1,037	206	77,932	19,911
New Jersey	84	12	1,621	342	160,737	44,444
New Mexico	72	11	734	240	109,297	35,712
New York	502	52	9,734	1,927	835,147	258,055
North Carolina	304	34	5,428	1,059	688,691	160,961
North Dakota	86	8	1,125	207	92,576	18,993
Ohio	477	53	10,728	2,771	863,874	214,994
Oklahoma	232	28	5,556	1,209	463,726	95,364
Oregon	219	24	2,768	718	336,278	69,062
Pennsylvania	933	92	17,401	2,585	1,581,058	276,321
Rhode Island	13	2	184	45	13,766	4,278
South Carolina	166	23	4,025	1,294	253,796	115,579
South Dakota	90	8	1,208	233	87,120	15,955
Tennessee	284	34	6,318	1,224	481,767	114,181
Texas	996	108	13,896	1,937	2,048,671	462,353
Utah	154	18	1,884	530	332,629	76,446
Vermont	57	6	1,068	157	69,059	15,885
Virginia	360	47	6,649	1,156	493,125	110,305
Washington	187	25	2,385	563	389,792	117,244
West Virginia	200	21	3,602	578	325,688	116,172
Wisconsin	652	53	9,998	1,316	1,329,161	272,105
Wyoming	52	6	604	149	89,832	29,427

Table D-3. Approximate Standard Errors of Resident Away-From-Home Participants, Days of Away-From-Home Participants by State Residents, and Trip-Related Expenditures for Away-From-Home Activities by State Residents

(Numbers in thousands)

State	Participation		Days		Expenditures in dollars	
	Estimate	Standard error	Estimate	Standard error	Estimate	Standard error
Alabama	348	50	7,301	3,047	198,132	61,485
Alaska	68	13	1,492	520	65,576	27,602
Arizona	381	42	4,554	886	301,997	75,465
Arkansas	304	46	4,253	1,372	70,098	25,680
California	2,565	200	46,538	8,681	2,226,634	504,935
Colorado	531	67	7,548	1,984	303,943	83,737
Connecticut	290	33	4,987	1,043	240,708	61,745
Delaware	49	8	811	276	12,490	3,833
Florida	988	119	13,180	3,390	455,521	105,349
Georgia	371	71	4,934	1,761	289,920	122,816
Hawaii	55	10	485	124	30,005	10,851
Idaho	183	32	2,876	805	87,351	28,403
Illinois	756	92	7,366	1,477	431,477	115,300
Indiana	611	72	7,894	1,650	234,756	61,310
Iowa	344	51	4,233	867	104,542	33,072
Kansas	234	31	3,427	1,156	91,838	28,745
Kentucky	540	68	3,978	835	163,835	45,402
Louisiana	234	42	3,536	1,038	118,317	49,801
Maine	213	30	3,938	1,066	105,340	28,268
Maryland	305	43	4,841	1,310	103,265	25,729
Massachusetts	531	50	8,959	1,720	249,979	56,447
Michigan	827	127	10,455	3,288	522,877	153,343
Minnesota	579	92	9,010	2,413	458,934	162,740
Mississippi	145	35	1,391	421	77,767	27,913
Missouri	709	86	14,619	3,543	365,259	103,690
Montana	184	23	1,777	498	57,461	20,990
Nebraska	151	18	1,201	176	55,793	15,941
Nevada	168	26	1,912	479	108,053	42,601
New Hampshire	127	16	2,246	561	61,263	14,140
New Jersey	513	54	8,408	2,189	195,252	44,467
New Mexico	220	24	3,803	844	81,860	20,074
New York	1,178	147	13,927	2,835	887,039	240,941
North Carolina	402	59	3,544	1,035	324,968	105,504
North Dakota	30	8	278	120	8,290	3,921
Ohio	1,174	125	9,232	1,427	365,635	95,003
Oklahoma	414	60	7,930	3,634	291,664	81,739
Oregon	481	66	7,455	3,205	177,364	51,932
Pennsylvania	1,038	127	13,013	2,727	587,806	168,911
Rhode Island	96	10	1,207	293	44,400	11,412
South Carolina	332	46	2,222	471	167,464	44,431
South Dakota	116	17	709	143	46,769	14,583
Tennessee	725	82	14,819	4,776	242,507	73,041
Texas	1,176	206	31,689	12,769	922,669	360,407
Utah	255	36	3,063	817	116,401	32,391
Vermont	82	11	1,803	504	25,689	6,661
Virginia	603	81	6,888	1,850	154,992	39,913
Washington	686	56	8,918	1,333	314,680	69,667
West Virginia	129	31	3,205	1,345	83,475	37,348
Wisconsin	424	73	4,367	1,129	188,626	54,452
Wyoming	82	13	894	223	54,472	19,022

Table D-1. Parameters a and b for Calculating Approximate Standard Errors of Sportspersons, Anglers, Hunters, and Wildlife-Watching Participants

(These parameters are to be used only to calculate estimates of standard errors for characteristics developed from the screening sample)

State	6 years old and older		6- to 15-year-olds only	
	a	b	a	b
United States	−0.000015	4,173	−0.000365	14,798
Alabama	−0.000523	2,173	−0.014402	8,642
Alaska	−0.001157	697	−0.024644	2,566
Arizona	−0.000399	2,178	−0.008468	7,441
Arkansas	−0.001116	2,820	−0.026111	9,698
California	−0.000126	4,134	−0.003139	16,914
Colorado	−0.000573	2,435	−0.019382	12,522
Connecticut	−0.000313	1,005	−0.008787	4,151
Delaware	−0.000510	396	−0.014882	1,597
Florida	−0.000266	4,389	−0.006122	13,852
Georgia	−0.000568	4,653	−0.012587	16,121
Hawaii	−0.000437	517	−0.009528	1,602
Idaho	−0.001346	1,759	−0.042091	8,654
Illinois	−0.000296	3,416	−0.007029	12,542
Indiana	−0.000488	2,782	−0.012165	10,911
Iowa	−0.000762	2,062	−0.020347	7,491
Kansas	−0.000537	1,329	−0.016690	6,138
Kentucky	−0.000772	2,935	−0.018308	9,902
Louisiana	−0.000775	3,143	−0.017795	11,036
Maine	−0.000924	1,135	−0.030300	4,683
Maryland	−0.000357	1,821	−0.008162	6,298
Massachusetts	−0.000261	1,521	−0.007130	5,692
Michigan	−0.000685	6,318	−0.018937	26,784
Minnesota	−0.001009	4,733	−0.029835	20,037
Mississippi	−0.000757	1,982	−0.016992	6,865
Missouri	−0.000670	3,534	−0.018329	13,847
Montana	−0.001418	1,227	−0.033110	3,719
Nebraska	−0.000567	902	−0.014086	3,277
Nevada	−0.000515	1,159	−0.011577	4,097
New Hampshire	−0.000535	650	−0.015945	2,744
New Jersey	−0.000209	1,655	−0.005070	6,099
New Mexico	−0.000620	1,097	−0.016872	4,557
New York	−0.000320	5,582	−0.009275	22,967
North Carolina	−0.000416	3,286	−0.011916	14,068
North Dakota	−0.001096	637	−0.036240	2,677
Ohio	−0.000484	5,045	−0.011219	17,172
Oklahoma	−0.000744	2,389	−0.020948	9,767
Oregon	−0.000752	2,533	−0.024824	11,839
Pennsylvania	−0.000544	6,176	−0.014615	22,903
Rhode Island	−0.000315	308	−0.008710	1,182
South Carolina	−0.000560	2,174	−0.016004	9,034
South Dakota	−0.001061	745	−0.025331	2,568
Tennessee	−0.000565	3,084	−0.015267	11,667
Texas	−0.000466	9,557	−0.011141	38,300
Utah	−0.000700	1,541	−0.018090	7,116
Vermont	−0.001053	611	−0.032724	2,420
Virginia	−0.000450	3,102	−0.014313	14,311
Washington	−0.000349	2,031	−0.010251	8,539
West Virginia	−0.001092	1,823	−0.042234	8,929
Wisconsin	−0.000820	4,156	−0.021060	15,086
Wyoming	−0.001268	592	−0.028116	1,742

Table D-5. Parameters a and b for Calculating Approximate Standard Errors of Levels for the Detailed Sportspersons Sample

State	Sportspersons and anglers 16 years old and older		Hunters 16 years old and older	
	a	b	a	b
United States............................	**−0.000027**	**6,125**	**−0.000025**	**5,756**
Alabama..............................	−0.000936	3,324	−0.000921	3,268
Alaska...............................	−0.002197	1,096	−0.002013	1,004
Arizona..............................	−0.000641	2,941	−0.000403	1,849
Arkansas............................	−0.001833	3,951	−0.001705	3,674
California............................	−0.000239	6,523	−0.000213	5,801
Colorado............................	−0.000960	3,459	−0.000735	2,650
Connecticut..........................	−0.000545	1,490	−0.000514	1,407
Delaware............................	−0.000758	507	−0.000720	482
Florida..............................	−0.000415	5,911	−0.000347	4,943
Georgia.............................	−0.000965	6,668	−0.000752	5,199
Hawaii..............................	−0.000763	774	−0.000751	761
Idaho...............................	−0.002486	2,738	−0.001888	2,080
Illinois..............................	−0.000430	4,201	−0.000388	3,789
Indiana..............................	−0.000821	3,939	−0.000777	3,729
Iowa................................	−0.001383	3,234	−0.001535	3,589
Kansas..............................	−0.001097	2,315	−0.001433	3,024
Kentucky............................	−0.001222	3,983	−0.001048	3,415
Louisiana............................	−0.001300	4,464	−0.001271	4,365
Maine...............................	−0.001560	1,675	−0.001469	1,578
Maryland............................	−0.000552	2,392	−0.000456	1,975
Massachusetts........................	−0.000412	2,072	−0.000383	1,929
Michigan.............................	−0.001085	8,470	−0.001214	9,474
Minnesota...........................	−0.001694	6,812	−0.001504	6,049
Mississippi...........................	−0.001355	3,000	−0.001169	2,588
Missouri.............................	−0.001031	4,662	−0.001067	4,825
Montana.............................	−0.002523	1,899	−0.002383	1,793
Nebraska............................	−0.001066	1,449	−0.001236	1,680
Nevada..............................	−0.000898	1,703	−0.000823	1,561
New Hampshire.......................	−0.000801	836	−0.000774	808
New Jersey...........................	−0.000327	2,200	−0.000251	1,690
New Mexico..........................	−0.001323	1,984	−0.001264	1,895
New York............................	−0.000456	6,842	−0.000378	5,671
North Carolina........................	−0.000713	4,794	−0.000588	3,951
North Dakota.........................	−0.001558	791	−0.001754	890
Ohio................................	−0.000851	7,569	−0.000697	6,194
Oklahoma............................	−0.001278	3,504	−0.001303	3,574
Oregon..............................	−0.001291	3,730	−0.001024	2,957
Pennsylvania.........................	−0.000867	8,490	−0.001030	10,089
Rhode Island.........................	−0.000487	410	−0.000425	358
South Carolina........................	−0.000983	3,259	−0.000981	3,251
South Dakota.........................	−0.001728	1,038	−0.001532	920
Tennessee...........................	−0.001019	4,790	−0.000929	4,367
Texas...............................	−0.000859	14,660	−0.000725	12,388
Utah................................	−0.001453	2,627	−0.001268	2,292
Vermont.............................	−0.001514	766	−0.001403	710
Virginia.............................	−0.000885	5,215	−0.001105	6,510
Washington...........................	−0.000626	3,116	−0.000676	3,368
West Virginia.........................	−0.001844	2,688	−0.001712	2,496
Wisconsin............................	−0.001281	5,572	−0.001144	4,978
Wyoming.............................	−0.003226	1,306	−0.002251	911

Table D-6. Parameters a, b, and c for Calculating Approximate Standard Errors for Expenditures for the Detailed Sportspersons Sample

State	Sportspersons and anglers 16 years old and older			Hunters 16 years old and older		
	a	b	c	a	b	c
United States...........................	**0.000118**	**−150,479**	**22,234**	**0.000918**	**−401,912**	**17,005**
Alabama...............................	0.019700	−12,417	5,855	0.016799	−96,800	6,317
Alaska.................................	0.030420	−2,004	1,057	0.031018	−14,867	1,091
Arizona................................	0.036222	−2,002	2,994	0.069395	−74,101	2,742
Arkansas..............................	0.024408	−27,794	6,433	0.010107	−101,205	7,942
California.............................	0.018462	−35,800	10,686	0.027550	−58,262	9,255
Colorado..............................	0.008867	676	5,062	0.034102	−27,935	4,373
Connecticut...........................	0.036498	−11,421	2,841	0.096937	−60,991	2,564
Delaware..............................	0.031385	−1,643	734	0.018489	−3,855	719
Florida................................	0.014951	−23,048	9,553	0.021932	−407,268	10,425
Georgia................................	0.022339	−47,820	8,031	0.051440	−143,590	7,061
Hawaii................................	0.065152	−5,771	830	0.123487	−5,097	588
Idaho.................................	0.034640	9,981	3,224	0.023728	−69,369	3,841
Illinois................................	0.017187	6,704	5,219	0.024778	74,958	3,321
Indiana...............................	0.027022	−16,160	4,558	0.042674	−61,618	4,557
Iowa..................................	0.033205	22,341	2,171	0.045665	−41,343	1,583
Kansas................................	0.034206	−23,245	3,454	0.042600	−116,049	4,343
Kentucky..............................	0.051496	−17,125	5,942	0.025277	−89,098	6,822
Louisiana.............................	0.023308	−66,118	7,237	0.027891	135,631	6,412
Maine.................................	0.022050	−7,457	2,175	0.021630	−12,360	2,038
Maryland..............................	0.015599	−14,663	3,208	0.018873	−30,982	2,820
Massachusetts.........................	0.049013	−25,362	3,792	0.138120	−47,649	2,049
Michigan..............................	0.035078	−148,672	13,535	0.039658	−147,585	12,587
Minnesota.............................	0.028185	−92,976	11,279	0.027553	−263,285	12,919
Mississippi............................	0.026713	−53,218	5,433	0.014058	−97,282	6,390
Missouri..............................	0.011821	−40,950	10,804	−0.005607	−190,726	17,070
Montana..............................	0.024760	−9,845	2,520	0.020119	−99,543	3,580
Nebraska..............................	0.018618	1,031	1,640	0.022265	−22,187	1,472
Nevada...............................	0.048609	−9,688	1,387	0.102222	−32,513	1,074
New Hampshire........................	0.025253	−6,176	1,434	0.037780	−26,900	1,448
New Jersey............................	0.019672	−39,093	4,262	0.029909	−90,209	3,910
New Mexico...........................	0.084483	2,232	1,181	0.096226	20,132	683
New York..............................	0.039569	−84,193	13,133	0.069695	−128,553	12,761
North Carolina........................	0.029775	−35,783	6,154	0.035333	−15,128	5,717
North Dakota..........................	0.033611	−586	751	0.032562	6,176	804
Ohio..................................	0.031480	−41,813	11,082	0.040646	−140,259	8,710
Oklahoma.............................	0.023920	−27,206	4,719	0.020041	−31,920	5,066
Oregon................................	0.029208	−11,360	5,033	0.019440	−76,401	4,937
Pennsylvania...........................	0.011981	−92,207	15,295	0.014951	−17,951	14,434
Rhode Island..........................	0.033545	−2,922	634	0.053976	−12,463	565
South Carolina........................	0.082716	−96,641	6,922	0.191600	−23,834	2,573
South Dakota..........................	0.030933	682	1,071	0.018421	−25,518	1,356
Tennessee.............................	0.027200	67,423	6,450	0.029272	−98,688	7,535
Texas.................................	0.032817	−69,604	20,795	0.027826	−146,956	22,831
Utah..................................	0.033896	−13,369	2,671	0.024936	−195,230	4,439
Vermont...............................	0.022379	−4,177	1,337	0.026395	−21,534	1,476
Virginia...............................	0.035897	−28,532	5,705	0.032298	−68,680	6,293
Washington............................	0.026464	−45,106	5,612	0.081551	81,860	1,611
West Virginia..........................	0.086611	−39,384	2,945	0.103915	−184,675	4,610
Wisconsin.............................	0.017762	−81,329	10,849	0.029543	−54,069	8,015
Wyoming..............................	0.075474	−5,404	1,197	0.090886	12,235	847

Table D-7. Parameters a, b, and c for Calculating Approximate Standard Errors for Days or Trips for the Detailed Sportspersons Sample

State	Sportspersons and anglers 16 years old and older			Hunters 16 years old and older		
	a	b	c	a	b	c
United States..........................	0.000211	−23,610	23,157	−0.000235	−85,241	22,698
Alabama.................................	0.027360	−4,011	4,995	0.035544	−6,621	5,383
Alaska..................................	0.016117	−432	1,681	0.027498	8	1,622
Arizona.................................	0.065842	−511	1,775	0.053516	−8,367	2,773
Arkansas................................	0.013952	−12,325	8,675	0.024038	−5,931	6,861
California	0.010707	−16,022	13,917	0.028439	−23,877	12,350
Colorado................................	0.019267	4,638	3,198	0.017940	128	3,608
Connecticut.............................	0.034363	−781	1,504	0.024306	−1,047	1,829
Delaware................................	0.061308	−234	527	0.058226	−184	529
Florida	0.010264	−17,862	11,170	0.022310	21,695	5,794
Georgia.................................	0.040208	−10,805	6,234	0.044845	16,702	1,853
Hawaii	0.034563	−1,603	1,552	0.212584	−1,169	945
Idaho...................................	0.069064	−15,482	4,996	0.024568	−5,756	3,301
Illinois.................................	0.005932	−8,487	9,365	0.001562	−38,372	13,100
Indiana.................................	0.006553	−5,775	6,973	0.018011	−6,028	6,053
Iowa....................................	0.026962	−7,704	4,252	0.037766	−10,398	4,032
Kansas	0.015744	−2,510	4,078	0.046706	−21,946	6,195
Kentucky	0.015099	−6,026	7,313	−0.014871	−7,130	8,307
Louisiana	0.004012	−4,767	6,568	0.022152	−3,240	5,213
Maine	0.030520	−7,661	3,270	0.003096	−10,278	3,842
Maryland	0.017639	−6,240	3,697	0.011515	−6,512	3,608
Massachusetts...........................	0.027491	−3,619	4,355	0.044116	−8,700	5,301
Michigan................................	0.011920	−23,905	20,643	0.025076	23,642	7,030
Minnesota...............................	0.035500	−7,447	10,504	0.027723	−23,061	14,333
Mississippi	0.015625	−10,362	5,357	−0.000218	−2,695	4,394
Missouri	0.019454	−11,342	12,042	0.010034	−70,146	19,451
Montana	0.018290	−1,849	2,202	0.013948	−3,887	2,640
Nebraska................................	0.009103	−2,063	3,655	−0.005553	−28,329	7,091
Nevada	0.043203	−1,733	1,536	0.123560	535	425
New Hampshire..........................	0.019444	−2,643	1,627	0.013722	400	1,313
New Jersey..............................	0.026108	1,903	1,969	0.013215	−1,967	2,735
New Mexico.............................	0.112638	−431	817	0.096905	807	610
New York...............................	0.029022	−22,367	14,881	0.008095	−27,096	17,017
North Carolina	0.021276	−6,354	5,499	0.012831	−28,563	9,265
North Dakota	0.019007	−3,002	1,621	0.008541	−5,760	2,617
Ohio....................................	0.022273	−21,768	15,604	0.044683	−9,949	10,955
Oklahoma...............................	0.006405	−10,237	8,296	0.013165	−12,426	8,445
Oregon	0.073495	−1,650	3,786	0.042692	−10,309	6,182
Pennsylvania............................	0.027085	−24,417	16,685	−0.014656	−134,270	41,466
Rhode Island	0.011732	−506	680	0.021282	−344	525
South Carolina	0.014487	−6,537	6,823	0.086503	1,677	2,737
South Dakota	0.012863	−1,152	1,751	0.019075	−2,901	1,859
Tennessee	0.005611	−9,561	11,404	−0.011681	−60,797	16,711
Texas...................................	0.014288	−13,795	18,462	−0.003611	−31,876	25,228
Utah	0.041500	−1,853	2,544	0.071790	3,964	792
Vermont	0.016042	−1,485	1,360	−0.006963	−2,952	1,792
Virginia.................................	0.008112	−5,920	7,627	0.011922	165	6,590
Washington..............................	0.017168	−6,558	4,800	0.045009	3,663	1,723
West Virginia	0.006512	−2,872	4,433	0.001964	−2,897	4,911
Wisconsin...............................	0.009197	−14,330	10,587	−0.002285	−35,565	15,098
Wyoming	0.025766	−1,835	1,823	0.034258	−3,738	1,705

Table D-8. Parameters a and b for Calculating Approximate Standard Errors of Levels of Wildlife Watching Participants for the Detailed Wildlife-Watching Sample

State	Away-from-home participants		Wildlife-watching participants[1]	
	a	b	a	b
United States..	**−0.000064**	**14,628**	**−0.000058**	**13,319**
Alabama...	−0.002522	8,955	−0.002252	7,994
Alaska..	−0.005091	2,539	−0.005744	2,864
Arizona...	−0.001212	5,555	−0.001128	5,170
Arkansas..	−0.003685	7,943	−0.003787	8,163
California...	−0.000633	17,272	−0.000632	17,247
Colorado..	−0.002818	10,157	−0.002773	9,995
Connecticut...	−0.001942	5,313	−0.001578	4,317
Delaware..	−0.002431	1,625	−0.002061	1,378
Florida...	−0.001067	15,191	−0.001082	15,396
Georgia...	−0.002273	15,705	−0.002082	14,383
Hawaii	−0.002169	2,200	−0.002077	2,106
Idaho...	−0.005872	6,469	−0.006027	6,640
Illinois...	−0.001350	13,189	−0.001237	12,083
Indiana...	−0.002090	10,031	−0.002026	9,722
Iowa	−0.003442	8,051	−0.003725	8,712
Kansas	−0.002087	4,403	−0.002245	4,737
Kentucky	−0.003921	12,780	−0.003130	10,201
Louisiana	−0.002878	9,878	−0.002325	7,980
Maine	−0.005383	5,779	−0.005003	5,372
Maryland	−0.001401	6,072	−0.001512	6,552
Massachusetts.......................................	−0.001153	5,803	−0.001045	5,260
Michigan..	−0.003188	24,879	−0.002805	21,892
Minnesota...	−0.004869	19,579	−0.004257	17,116
Mississippi..	−0.004033	8,929	−0.004149	9,184
Missouri	−0.003241	14,653	−0.002731	12,349
Montana	−0.006536	4,919	−0.005006	3,768
Nebraska..	−0.001913	2,600	−0.001770	2,406
Nevada...	−0.003763	7,131	−0.002387	4,524
New Hampshire	−0.002265	2,364	−0.002070	2,160
New Jersey	−0.000942	6,346	−0.000899	6,057
New Mexico...	−0.002139	3,207	−0.002023	3,034
New York...	−0.001498	22,454	−0.001320	19,791
North Carolina	−0.001307	8,785	−0.001368	9,194
North Dakota	−0.004745	2,408	−0.004900	2,486
Ohio	−0.001834	16,302	−0.001729	15,365
Oklahoma...	−0.004720	12,946	−0.003724	10,214
Oregon...	−0.004482	12,948	−0.003771	10,895
Pennsylvania..	−0.001862	18,235	−0.001779	17,426
Rhode Island	−0.001588	1,338	−0.001451	1,222
South Carolina	−0.002527	8,378	−0.002147	7,118
South Dakota	−0.005879	3,532	−0.005273	3,168
Tennessee	−0.002040	9,583	−0.002340	10,996
Texas...	−0.002981	50,906	−0.002276	38,865
Utah	−0.002948	5,329	−0.003322	6,007
Vermont	−0.003834	1,940	−0.003687	1,866
Virginia...	−0.002142	12,625	−0.002049	12,078
Washington..	−0.001012	5,037	−0.001076	5,361
West Virginia	−0.005125	7,470	−0.005457	7,954
Wisconsin...	−0.002461	10,707	−0.003232	14,058
Wyoming	−0.006998	2,833	−0.006562	2,657

[1] Use these parameters for total wildlife-watching participants and around-the-home participants.

Table D-9. Parameters a, b, and c for Calculating Approximate Standard Errors for Expenditures and Days or Trips for Wildlife-Watching Participants

State	Expenditures			Days or trips		
	a	b	c	a	b	c
United States..........................	**0.000184**	**−1,140,662**	**67,137**	**0.000574**	**1,457,630**	**−8,497**
Alabama...............................	0.045588	−11,994	16,603	0.188740	−119,343	614
Alaska................................	0.120206	−27,366	3,041	−0.124071	−135,739	22,893
Arizona...............................	0.030207	−53,304	10,729	−0.012992	48,146	15,350
Arkansas..............................	0.099812	14,720	8,751	−0.017705	122,002	28,315
California	0.033850	−512,106	41,075	−0.045068	409,984	182,262
Colorado..............................	0.027999	−274,128	22,499	−0.048837	−38,813	65,367
Connecticut............................	0.021634	−65,691	10,399	−0.024457	−95,765	25,345
Delaware..............................	0.065106	−1,447	1,138	−0.008505	9,777	5,498
Florida	0.023886	346,119	21,198	0.008852	367,813	29,038
Georgia...............................	0.074762	−1,010,585	34,617	−0.043108	−269,579	83,544
Hawaii	0.083826	−21,578	2,574	−0.072050	−22,450	10,110
Idaho.................................	0.062974	−42,113	7,740	−0.034736	−28,632	22,517
Illinois................................	0.036256	−247,805	22,614	−0.015710	−127,759	55,397
Indiana	0.036663	−31,127	16,250	−0.011371	−60,979	38,357
Iowa	0.079272	54,459	5,841	−0.010582	−64,612	23,312
Kansas	0.065343	2,002	6,423	−0.009647	290,376	9,046
Kentucky	0.054215	7,733	10,118	−0.027046	−203,563	66,052
Louisiana	0.122208	−20,968	9,262	−0.027645	11,297	25,905
Maine	0.023874	−51,089	9,384	−0.124695	−361,658	61,734
Maryland	0.014472	−4,594	10,674	0.003905	125,364	13,230
Massachusetts..........................	0.028723	−178,823	9,836	−0.028071	−151,233	43,446
Michigan..............................	0.034044	−350,268	38,895	−0.189982	−1,478,372	355,858
Minnesota.............................	0.074185	−156,337	26,053	−0.037135	−287,075	81,476
Mississippi	0.069734	−5,671	8,343	0.007734	−4,828	12,669
Missouri	0.050350	−370,879	19,939	−0.072363	−297,324	107,372
Montana	0.096467	−101,441	7,127	0.021739	75,970	2,590
Nebraska..............................	0.057553	−29,126	3,150	−0.037603	−53,492	15,634
Nevada	0.114708	−32,736	5,704	0.007035	8,360	8,647
New Hampshire.........................	0.014724	−17,918	4,039	−0.004938	74,043	4,376
New Jersey............................	0.022949	−169,333	13,969	−0.040442	238,149	40,992
New Mexico............................	0.036652	16,768	4,306	−0.023441	72,449	11,803
New York	0.042036	−450,788	32,575	−0.019285	−366,511	102,534
North Carolina.........................	0.061423	−16,794	13,694	−0.012815	19,657	37,216
North Dakota	0.155007	−2,199	1,794	0.150664	6,024	376
Ohio	0.035458	−205,570	28,049	−0.018753	−103,758	63,267
Oklahoma..............................	0.036357	−21,977	15,171	−0.000564	1,344,926	16,961
Oregon	0.062814	−65,011	9,965	−0.004734	831,881	37,513
Pennsylvania...........................	0.054585	−176,791	24,331	−0.024636	−296,844	94,825
Rhode Island	0.037242	−31	2,537	−0.019391	234	7,490
South Carolina	0.017341	−52,304	14,141	−0.021836	−45,588	28,960
South Dakota	0.058011	−16,346	3,878	−0.063876	−12,873	14,245
Tennessee	0.058962	−19,581	19,197	−0.067979	539,487	98,190
Texas.................................	0.107126	268,978	41,639	−0.115263	−2,660,430	425,213
Utah	0.056246	−5,750	4,842	−0.002938	−77,345	25,347
Vermont	0.005556	−22,018	4,065	−0.014449	33,588	6,073
Virginia...............................	0.043764	−51,970	12,817	−0.046070	−227,508	91,189
Washington............................	0.030615	−16,210	11,199	−0.000250	36,174	12,719
West Virginia	0.118586	−4,653	8,819	−0.073404	38,459	30,640
Wisconsin..............................	0.009997	−400,732	26,411	−0.015178	−125,383	46,927
Wyoming	0.083907	−31,350	3,012	−0.062286	−29,913	12,976